From: Tony

To: Eddie
— /07/2003

I Speak FOR THE PEOPLE

ERROR ON PAGE 15.

I Speak FOR THE PEOPLE

THE MEMOIRS OF WYNTER CRAWFORD

Edited by Woodville K. Marshall

Ian Randle Publishers
Kingston

First published in Jamaica, 2003 by
Ian Randle Publishers
11 Cunningham Avenue
www.ianrandlepublishers.com

© estate of Wynter Crawford

ISBN 976-637-126-1 (Paperback)
ISBN 976-637-123-7 (Hardback)

A catalogue record of this book is available from the National Library of Jamaica

Book and cover design by Errol Stennett
Printed and bound in the United States of America

CONTENTS

FOREWORD

BY
GEORGE LAMMING

Historians are often rebuked for their failure or reluctance to consider the historical context in which political figures may have been coerced into making compromises which seemed prudent for the time. Here, context assumes a certain authority, and it is even elevated to the criterion by which we are asked to judge the writer's objectivity. But the primary significance of context may also serve as a form of apologetics intended to shield or preserve the memory of a historical figure whom time has rewarded with the status of hero. The current argument around Lord Nelson's statue as an appropriate symbol of national affirmation in Barbados may offer an example of this tension. Vital as context may be, it deserves no greater claim on our attention than the judgement which is influenced by some profound change in our mode of perceiving a particular reality. Change in our way of seeing is no less a source of moral authority which may require each generation to forge its own interpretation of the complex of failure and achievement which constitutes its inheritance.

This is the kind of intellectual challenge which the memoirs of the late Wynter Crawford trigger some forty years after his formal retirement from the political career that was a watershed in the making of the modern Barbados. There is such an impressive catalogue of initiatives recorded in his name (the flour mill, the cotton knitting/spinning industry, the cement factory, the National Insurance Scheme, the East Coast Road, etc.) that it could be argued that his was, perhaps, the most alert and incisive political imagination at work for more than a decade, from 1940 when he first entered the parliament as elected member for St. Philip until the mid-1950s after his own Congress Party had collapsed, and he formed an alliance with the Democratic Labour Party under the late Errol Barrow.

Today his name does not make any distinctive signature on the landscape. This omission has the weight of a public embarrassment which demands some urgent correction, especially at a time when there are official appeals to reclaim the past and repair the historical amnesia which has deprived a post-Independence generation of a conscious connection with a period and a political figure so critical to its social and cultural formation.

Born in 1910, Crawford's childhood and adolescence would have been lived in a society where Parliament existed without any of the humanising constraints of a popular democracy. Less than four percent of the adult population had the vote; and this level of disenfranchisement would have persisted until as late as 1943, or almost twenty-five years before Independence. The requirements of the suffrage had reduced the majority of the population to being strangers at the gate.

The locations of power would have been rigorously contained within the interests and authority of a white planter/merchant economic elite. It would have been rare to find among such a ruling class any inclination or genuine regard for intellectual distinction. That class cultivated without apology an appetite for wealth which was measured largely by ownership of land and, later, by the exclusive appropriation of almost all sectors of commerce. It proposed and facilitated by law arrangements for import and export trade. The official church and school and all institutions created for the purpose of social control were designed to ensure the supremacy of this elite. Constitutional change was a tedious and provocative mockery of any genuine reform; and, when the temperature of feeling among the impoverished majority of the population exploded in the Riots of 1937, a new chapter in political negotiation had begun.

It was this event which triggered Crawford's ambition to play some significant role in national politics. He had already launched his weekly newspaper, the *Observer*, in 1934, and had inherited a reading constituency among the working poor who had formerly relied on the guidance of the radical journalist, Clennell Wickham, and the Barbados *Herald* which Wickham edited. The *Herald* was political descriptive writing and character analysis of a very high order; and the stubborn dignity of Wickham made the newspaper all the more vulnerable to the racial fury of the white merchant class. In 1930, the *Herald* was the casualty of a libel suit which forced a change of ownership and ultimately drove Wickham into exile and silence. The liberation working-class struggles which had been pioneered by Charles Duncan O'Neale in the 1920s would be taken up as the recurring theme of Crawford's *Observer*. This newspaper would have contributed significantly to the formation of a working-class intellectual leadership.

The language of Crawford's memorandum to the Moyne Commission, January 21, 1939, not only carries the weight of every worker's complaint, but is informed by an ideological conceptualising of the struggles which characterised the third decade of the 20th century. The tone of that memorandum must have taken the Commission by surprise. His emphasis is the nature of colonial rule:

> It is high time that this infamous tyranny, this system of fascism better known as colonial imperialism, should be completely destroyed. There is no name too evil to be applied to a system which keeps thousands of workers in semi-starvation, denies them all human rights, and crushes with brutal military force any effort on their part to lift their standards of life . . .

Sir Edward Stubbs, a member of the Commission, quickly detected where this was leading, and made the limits of his agenda quite clear. He said bluntly: 'I do not think I will discuss the first part of your memorandum which deals with the evils of Imperialism and Fascism . . .'

The memorandum, like the *Observer*, provided evidence of an editor with a lively curiosity about international affairs. The year 1936 was a notorious landmark which recalled the revolt by General Franco against the Spanish Republic and the intervention by Germany and Italy on behalf of the Fascist insurgents in Spain. After three years of a bloody civil war – and a million dead – the Fascists under Franco came to power. That would have been 1939, the year of the Moyne Commission's visit to investigate the causes of the Riots. But the *Observer* would also have been a constant source of information on the Italian invasion of Ethiopia in 1935, just a year before the outbreak of the Spanish Civil War. This violation of the sovereignty of the ancient Kingdom of Ethiopia had aroused the greatest hostility throughout the African diaspora and had electrified a dormant Caribbean/African connection which had been propagated by Marcus Garvey. A perilous reality had been achieved by the Garveyite ideology of *Race first*; and the movement acquired a degree of authenticity that it had been often denied.

Crawford does not admit to any Garveyite influence; and the African connection for him remains a strictly colonial question of international dimensions. There was an exchange of newspapers between him and the Nigerian, Dr. Nnamdi Azikiwe, who had founded the *African Post* in 1934 and the *West African Pilot*, Lagos in 1937. Azikiwe would become the first president of the Federal Republic of Nigeria in 1960. Neither Azikiwe nor Crawford would have anticipated in 1937 that, some eleven years later, their newspapers, the *West African Pilot* and the *Observer*, would have collaborated in the attack on Grantley Adams for his defence of British colonial rule before a meeting of the U.N. General Assembly in Paris in October 1948. The severe condemnation of Adams by the *West African Pilot* must have come as a boon to Crawford who carried the text in the *Observer* as part of his own local vendetta with Adams:

> Mr. Adams ought to know that the overall policy of the Colonial Office stands condemned before all men of goodwill. Mr. Adams, by his irresponsible and inspired utterances put into his ignoble mouth by his British masters, has dealt a wicked blow at all suffering peoples . . .

It would now appear to be unfortunate that Adams had been manoeuvred into an assignment from which he would never recover his integrity as an authentic anti-colonial leader. Nor would Crawford's international connections have come to his rescue. The frequent citations in the *Observer* from *Tass* confirm Crawford's access to a correspondent in Russia; and he also received bulletins from the great Pan-Africanist leader, George Padmore, who had lived in the Soviet Union and was resident in London during the late 1930s.

It is this radical and internationalist perspective which may have put him at odds with rivals and colleagues who were more accommodating to the requirements of the Barbadian society. References to his own ancestry are much preoccupied with gradations of colour as an index of social privilege or personal misfortune. Discrimination against the colour Black in all its manifestations has always been a toxic feature of social relations in all Caribbean societies. But it is in Barbados that the racial contract of white dominance and black accommodation had been experienced in its most extreme form. Among a people haunted by the fear of racial insult, even where racial miscegenation is the norm, among a people always nervous about its location in the social hierarchy, Crawford's memoirs portray a man of amazing social confidence, with an unalterable conviction of his self-worth. It is important to remind readers that in 1944 and again in 1946 the electoral success of his Congress Party gave Crawford a certain national stature which made it seem more than a likelihood that he was destined to be a future Prime Minister of Barbados. He was then the major rival to Grantley Adams for the leadership of the Barbados masses. And whereas Adams had evolved from the tutelage of those who urged gradual reform and a temporary alliance with the ruling elite, Crawford had been shaped by the climate of a more radical opinion created by Charles Duncan O'Neale and Clennell Wickham.

If a radical thrust for reform reflected the general mood and aspirations of the times, we are invited to speculate on questions which the memoirs raise without offering very persuasive answers. Why, for example, did the Congress Party collapse the way it did while the Barbados Labour Party endures and makes no apology for regarding itself as the glorious legacy of Grantley Adams?

While it is true that levels of financial support are decisive in determining the result of elections in a capitalist democracy, it must be a matter of concern to literate citizens that the space for independent thought that is committed to a vision of society which rejects the attainment of high standards of living as the *raison d'etre* of human existence – such space is shrinking with the dictatorial authority of the communications media and the anaesthetising designs of the entertainment industry.

Crawford gives some alarming accounts of the lack of any consensual discourse in arriving at who would be the first leader of the victorious DLP in 1961. And his report of the dissolution of talks that were intended to finalise agreement on a Federation of the Little Eight renews for me the question whether the Caribbean soil has yet become receptive to democratic practice.

The memoirs return Crawford to the society in his own voice and allow us to experience the immediate force of his personality – confident, courageous and assertive in situations which others might have approached with greater caution. He has rendered an invaluable service to his biographers who will now have a much clearer view of those areas of a public life which deserve to be explored and shared with present and future generations.

ACKNOWLEDGEMENTS

As would be expected, the production of a work such as this could not have been accomplished without the help and support of numerous persons. It may therefore not be feasible to mention them all individually but we shall try to do so for those persons, organisations and agencies that made especially significant contributions.

First, our deep gratitude must be extended to Woodville Marshall whose transcripts of interviews with Mr Crawford formed the basis of these memoirs and for his role as editor of the volume. Next, I must mention Mrs Monica Martineau Skeete who undertook the editorial task of transforming those transcripts and the supplementary information dictated by Mr Crawford into narrative form. Third, I must notice Dr DeLisle Crawford, brother of Wynter Crawford, for his management of this project and his contribution of the epilogue to the book.

Another key person in the enterprise is Mr Harold Hoyte, friend and admirer of Mr Crawford, who, in his role as Founder, President and CEO of the Nation Publishing Company, Ltd., fully delivered on his promise to Wynter to provide corporate sponsorship for the publication of this book. He also read the early versions of the manuscript and provided copious written notes and comments for its improvement.

Our thanks and gratitude are also owed to:

Sir Theodore Brancker and Mr C.B. Williams (both now deceased) for personal interviews; Dame Elsie Pilgrim, Dr John Gilmore and Mrs Kathleen Gilmore who gave of their time to edit and advise on earlier drafts of the manuscript; and also to Robert (Bobby) Clarke who, at short notice, also commented on later versions of the manuscript.

The following departments of government and other organisations provided photographic or written material:

The Barbados Department of Archives, with special reference to Mrs Christine Matthews-Rocheford, Chief Archivist.

The Government Information Service (GIS) with special reference to Mrs Margaret Hope, Chief Information Officer, and her assistants Ms Lynn Lucas and Mr Lennox Edwards.

Ministry of Education, Audio-Visual Department, with special reference to Mr Selwyn Belle, Head, Ms Arlette St. Hill, Ms Glenda Watson and Mr David Waterman;

The Barbados Museum and Historical Society, with special reference to Ms Alissandra Cummins, Director, and assistants Ms Angela Boyce, Mr James Marshall and Mr Kevin Farmer;

The National Library Service, with special reference to Ms Annette Smith, Director; University of the West Indies (UWI) Library, Cave Hill Campus; The Barbados Advocate Publishing Company, with special reference to Ms Norville, Librarian; The Nation Publishing Company, with special reference to Mr Charles Grant, photographer.

The following individuals and families were kind enough to make loans of photographic material:

The Jack Martineau family (Mrs Myrna Taitt)

The James A. Tudor family (Mrs Grace Jordan, Mrs Elsie Burrowes)

Lady J.E.T. Branker, Mrs Cyrilene Gale

Mr F.H. Godson (grandson of the late Rev. F. Godson)

Mrs Idalia Roche (sister of Wynter Crawford)

We also thank Mr Ronnie Hughes and Dr Curtis Jacobs for research and Mr Tony Hinds for providing advice and historical information.

There are three other special persons whom we must recognise for their sterling contributions over the last two to three years to the direct and indirect promotion of this book: Mr Albert Maynard, one of the columnists of *The Nation*, for his in-depth full-page tributes to Wynter Crawford on the Crawford birth-date anniversary; Mr Alfred Pragnell, popular host of a Voice of Barbados programme, who has done similarly on his radio programme; Mr David Commisiong, Director of the Commission for Pan-African Affairs who, in addition to staging a large public assembly tribute in 2000, frequently pays tribute to Crawford in his public presentations.

Thanks also to Mrs Shirley C. Walrond and Ms Sherry-Anne Toppin for typing.

Finally our thanks go to Mr George Lamming for accepting our invitation to write the foreword.

Cecil Crawford

INTRODUCTION

Wynter Algernon Crawford (1910–1993) was indisputably one of the giants of the movement for political and social enfranchisement that culminated in the independence of Barbados in 1966. While his career and achievements are usually compared with those of his outstanding contemporary, Grantley Herbert Adams, there is a case for seeing him in slightly different terms – less as the political rival of Adams and more as a social reformer and social activist in the tradition of Samuel Jackman Prescod and Clennell Wickham. To a large extent, this assessment can be illustrated by activities in his career as crusading journalist, as a radical politician and political party leader, and as Cabinet Minister and principled politician.

George Lamming has made the important point that Crawford's most enduring contribution may well have been his editing and publishing of the *Barbados Observer*. Crawford founded that weekly newspaper in 1934

Wynter Crawford as Minister of Government (1961–66) at his desk

when he was only twenty-four and, with hardly any professional assistance, he edited it for the entire forty-one years of its existence. The importance of this newspaper was that, particularly in its first twenty years of existence, it gave a clear voice to the concerns of the underprivileged in much the same way that Clennell Wickham's *Herald* had done during the 1920s. The *Observer* was a radical newspaper, boldly identifying and attacking 'conservative' forces and racial discrimination, vigorously promoting 'progressive' causes and the activities of progressive politicians like Grantley Adams (until mid-1939) and the members of the Congress Party, campaigning for a socialist rearrangement of society, for self-government and independence. Because of the nature of its analyses and prescriptions and its strident anti-colonial tone and content, the newspaper was both the *bête noire* of colonial administrators in the 1930s and 1940s **and** a vital element in that political and intellectual ferment that provoked fundamental social change in Barbados.

Crawford's career in representative politics spanned some twenty-six years (1940–66), the period during which he represented the parish of St. Philip in the House of Assembly. But his activity as a radical politician and political leader could be dated from 1937 to about 1951. At least three things stand out in that career. First is his contribution to political party organization. He, along with five or six others, founded in March 1938 the organization that eventually became known as the Barbados Labour Party (BLP); and he was actually asked to be it first secretary. Though his membership of that organization barely lasted a year because of his dissatisfaction with Adams's treatment of Herbert Seale and 'Chrissie' Brathwaite, Crawford must be given the credit for proposing to Hope Stevens that formal organization was a prerequisite for political and social change in Barbados. The second part of his contribution to party political organization was his founding of the West Indian National Congress Party in 1944, which survived with himself as its leader until 1956. This party quickly established itself as a political force mainly because of the energy, ideas and charisma of its leader, and it was fully a match for Grantley Adams's Barbados Labour Party in the elections of 1944 and 1946. Therefore it made a contribution to emerging party politics by offering a clear alternative on the left and by providing political education to the electorate through its sharp definition of issues and through its focus on the rural/agricultural sector. The third part of his contribution to political party organization was visible between 1951 and 1955. After the Congress Party's calamitous defeat in the 1951 general election, the first under universal adult suffrage, its three-man representation in the

House of Assembly operated as the core of opposition to which disaffected members of the Barbados Labour Party could attach themselves particularly after 1952.

The second important element in Crawford's career as a radical politician was the consistent articulation of a programme that was most radical at that time. From the early issues of the *Observer* through his period as an Independent in the House (1940–44) through his leadership of the Congress Party, he called for compulsory education, free books and hot lunches for school children, adult suffrage, a national health and unemployment scheme, state ownership of parts of the agricultural sector, and the disestablishment of the Anglican Church. Equally important, he and his party tried valiantly, particularly in 1944–46, to organize the agricultural workers. Recognizing that the bias of the Barbados Workers' Union (and the Barbados Labour Party) towards the port and urban workers led to neglect of the concerns of agricultural workers, he and the Congress Party established the Congress Union. While that union failed for lack of organizational and financial resources, its short-lived existence helped to ensure that the 1945 sugar strike would be settled on terms acceptable to the agricultural workers and that the Barbados Workers' Union would extend its mandate beyond Bridgetown.

The feud with Grantley Adams is the other main feature of Crawford's career as a radical politician. That feud gave form and texture to Barbadian politics from about 1939 until 1952 when the 'Young Turks' in the Barbados Labour Party, led by Errol Barrow, began to harass Grantley Adams. Why there was this long-running feud is difficult to determine. Both men were close associates from 1934 to 1938; and Adams was a regular contributor to the *Observer*. Both men had an active social conscience and shared a political orientation if not precise political objectives. Both men spoke for 'labour' and would have been fully conscious of the damage to the progressive cause that their open feuding would cause. Yet from 1939 onwards the rupture was plain for all to see, and it was punctuated not merely by fierce exchanges on the political platforms and in the House of Assembly but also by an extremely messy libel action in 1945. Perhaps personal animosity had developed, perhaps their ideological positions had diverged, but certainly they no longer trusted each other as men or politicians.

Two main consequences flowed from all this. First, their split prolonged the political influence of the conservatives and therefore slowed the advance towards the institution of internal self-government. To illustrate: the result of the 1944 and 1946 elections produced an almost even three-way split. This meant that, although 'labour' held two-thirds of the seats in the House of Assembly, it could not exercise control over the membership of the Executive Committee (which was effectively the Government). Second, Adams and Crawford (almost in the fashion of Norman Manley and Alexander Bustamante) challenged each other for the leadership of the mass of the population, and the issue was always in doubt particularly between 1944 and 1946 when the electorate gave virtually equal support to the parties led by the two men. So it must be emphasised that it was a toss-up whether Crawford or Adams would have been identified with the political emancipation that occurred in the 1940s. Why that did not happen and why Crawford's party disintegrated after 1947 are matters for some conjecture and certainly for research.

Crawford did not attain leadership of government, but he did get a belated opportunity to implement significant parts of the programme that he had outlined during the 1940s. This occurred during the first Democratic Labour Party (DLP) government when, between 1961 and 1965, he simultaneously held several key ministries (Trade, Industry, Labour and Development, Commerce, Tourism) and was also named as Deputy Premier. His status as a senior minister was clearly a recognition not only of his long experience as a parliamentarian and as an agitator for a variety of causes but also of his energy, intelligence and vision. Two of his achievements as Minister might be mentioned. The first is the National Insurance Scheme. While the activity of the Barbados Workers' Union was crucial to its adoption, the earliest and most persistent advocate of such a scheme was Wynter Crawford. From as early as June 1945, Crawford had drawn the attention of the government to the Beveridge Plan of Britain and had urged it to take appropriate local action; and he reiterated those points in December 1948, January 1949, in April 1953, and again in September 1957. It was entirely appropriate that in 1965 he should preside over the preparation of the Act which eventually established the National Insurance Scheme. The second example is industrial development. He almost certainly was the first person in the island to advocate the adoption of the Puerto Rican model of economic development. Establishing contact with Governor Munoz Marin of Puerto Rico, he consistently urged the adoption of industrial incentives legislation and the establishment of small-scale industries. Therefore, as Minister of Development after 1961, he played a crucial role in the formulation of the policy that created the various industrial estates and attracted several industries to the island. Similarly, the promotion of tourism and the infrastructural development like the draining of the Constitution Swamp and the construction of the East Coast Road were projects which he had proposed in the 1940s and 1950s, and these were executed during his tenure in the Cabinet. Therefore, that programme of economic diversification which characterised the first DLP government was as much his and the Congress Party's as it was the DLP's.

The circumstances of his departure from political life in 1965/66, though intriguing, do him credit. At one level, his resignation from the Cabinet and eventually from the DLP could be regarded as an issue of principle – the refusal to abandon a position to which most Cabinet colleagues had firmly committed themselves. If this was the case, then his resignation and that of Erskine Ward's over the DLP's decision to abandon the proposed 'Little Eight' federation and to opt for independence for Barbados was unique in Barbadian political annals, and is an example to be commended. However, while Crawford was an active regionalist in a broad, borderless but personal sense, there is little evidence to suggest that he was an ardent political federationist either in West Indian or 'Little Eight' terms. At the 1947 Montego Bay Conference, he seemed more interested in arguing for self-government than in supporting the cause of federation. Later, when the 'Little Eight' was proposed, he seemed to favour that arrangement less out of a sense of community with the Windward and Leeward Islands than out of an appreciation of the practical economic advantages that could redound to Barbados from the proposed grouping. So, at another

Old Age Pensioners

level, one is forced to wonder whether Crawford was declaring that he could not abide by decisions on an important issue that seemed to be arrived at capriciously, and he may have been suggesting that any leader who behaved in such a fashion could not command his support. In other words, there is at least the possibility that Crawford and Ward were repudiating Barrow's leadership of the DLP, and Crawford's later proposal that a new party should be formed with Ward as leader seems to support such a conjecture. In either case, Crawford's motives for resignation do not appear to be self-serving.

Whatever the truth of the matter, it is entirely a matter for regret that Crawford's departure from political life at the relatively early age of fifty-six did rob the Barbadian community of the voice and influence of one who was eminently qualified for the role of elder statesman. But the rules of the political game put him in an unenviable position. The DLP under Barrow would never have forgiven him for the apparent challenge to its leader; and most of the BLP's leadership could not easily forgive or forget bruising encounters with this robust political campaigner and acerbic critic. However, because Crawford virtually disappeared from view (and therefore dropped out of Barbadian consciousness) during the last twenty-seven years of his life, there is no reason to discount his importance to the profession of journalism and to the political life of his country. His memoirs are therefore a timely reminder of his stature and achievements.

The text of these Memoirs was mainly derived from transcripts of interviews that I conducted with the author in 1985/86. As would be expected, the format of an oral history interview and the preoccupations of the interviewer would have resulted in uneven coverage of several topics, a measure of repetition, and disjointedness in the flow of information. However, the late Monica Skeete, with minimal assistance from the incapacitated author, managed to shape this difficult material in such a way that a coherent story could emerge. She must therefore be commended for a most creative piece of editing. My own contribution to the preparation of this text is minor by comparison. I have refined some of the language, eliminated some of the obvious repetitions, corrected some errors of fact, rearranged some sections of the text, and added footnotes to clarify issues and supply biographical information on important individuals.

Woodville Marshall

CHAPTER 1

Growing Up

The sound of what appeared to be marching men and music drifted onto the backyard of the house in which our family lived on the main St Lawrence highway. I was watching from the back-step of the house as the maid hung out some laundry to dry. She grabbed me and raised me to her shoulder and made for the gateway to the house. I saw a straggly band of volunteers marching along and singing what afterwards grew to be the familiar *'The Kaiser's daughter sick in bed, parlez-vous', and 'It's a long way to Tipperary'*. His Britannic Majesty's Government had just declared war on the Kaiser's Germany and Barbados was demonstrating its military might! I was four years old.[1]

World War I and its aftermath made little or no impact on me. But, by World War II, I was editing and publishing the *Observer* and receiving daily and nightly dispatches from many of the main theatres of war, including the never-ending stream from *Tass* in Russia even before Russia entered the war.

The house in which we lived was situated near the Stream Gospel Hall at St Lawrence and belonged to my mother's family. Next to it was the more pretentious house of one of my mother's elder sisters, my aunt Constance, who had twice been married. Her portion of land was larger, extending down to the Graeme Hall swamp. She never cultivated it but kept it for grazing her animals – cows and a horse which transported her to town on business in a double buggy; carried her two children to school, the boy to Combermere and the girl to Queen's College; and also transported her second husband on his bird-shooting expeditions during the season.

My mother was the darkest in colour of all her sisters. Her father was a tall, hale, hardy man whose skin was so light in colour that he could easily have passed for a white man in any northern country. Apparently he had a penchant for black women – both his wives were black. I knew one of them whom we used to call Aunt Rose. She was an angel. I remember once, when I got a nasty gash on my foot from the catwire fencing around the St Lawrence school playground, my mother could not even look at it, so I used to go to Aunt Rose for dressing every morning until it healed.

I was sent to a private school at four and, at five, I was enrolled at St Lawrence Boys' School, which was only a few steps down the road from where I lived and across the road from where my grandfather lived. The headmaster was a Mr. Rogers. He was married to my mother's aunt. I remember hearing my mother say that, on Sundays, her grandfather would take the family to St Lawrence Church by horse and carriage, drop them home after church, and then spend the rest of the day with his lady-friend. She was a Miss Cottle, who lived further down the road in front of the Graeme Hall swamp. At one time he planted rice there. He and Miss Cottle had two children, both girls. One later married Mr. Rogers, the headmaster of my school. She was his second wife, and one of their children became a prominent solicitor in the city, Mr. Erskine Rogers. The other daughter married a Mr. Lynch, and their son, Louis Lynch, became a prominent athlete and the founder of the Modern High School which filled a great void in the educational system of the day. The Louis Lynch Stand at the stadium is named after him, and the government recently renamed the Roebuck Secondary School after him as well. Mrs. Rogers died fairly young, and Mrs. Lynch inherited the area of swamp land which Miss Cottle had inherited from my mother's grandfather.

I remember no outstanding incidents during my five years at St Lawrence Boys' School. Both Mr. Rogers and his assistant masters, Mr. Crick and Mr. Small, were very efficient, courteous to the children and diligent in their duties. At age ten, I won a scholarship to Combermere School and remained there for another five years. Combermere School was then adjacent to Queen's College in Constitution Road. In later years, when the extension of Queen's College became imperative, the Combermere buildings were absorbed by Queen's College and (as Combermere's enrolment had outgrown its cramped space) Combermere was shifted to new buildings at Roebuck Street (Weymouth) which are now utilized by the Transport Board. From there, Combermere School was eventually moved to its present location at Waterford.

Combermere provided an interesting experience. At that time, most of the boys and teachers, including the headmaster, Mr George Burton, were white. When Mr. Burton retired, he was succeeded by another white headmaster, Mr 'Gussie' Cox. There were only five coloured teachers: Mr 'Gladio' Wilson who taught mathematics in fourth form, Mr 'Graffie' Pilgrim, visiting master in mathematics, the Reverend Hall, another visiting master who taught Latin, Mr Victor Southwell, who headed the commercial class, and Mr Woodbine Ford who taught Spanish in the upper forms.[2] French was a compulsory subject but, after form two, a pupil could choose to drop Latin and take Spanish instead, an option which I chose. Mr Ford, who reportedly spoke eight languages, taught Spanish at Harrison College and was, in addition, the distinguished editor of a newspaper (the *Agricultural Reporter*) owned by Mr E.T. Racker.

A new boy at Combermere at that time faced two alternatives for his initiation as a pupil of that school. On the first half-day of the term, either he was taken by senior boys into the headmaster's orchard, which was at the front of the school, and flogged with tamarind rods, or he was taken across the road to Queen's Park and thrown fully clothed into the small artificial lake which the Park boasted. I was fully aware of these practices and made up my mind not to be subjected to either. I knew two senior boys: one was Norman Legall, who became Colonial Post Master General, and the other was Timothy Headley, who became a solicitor. I got one of them to lead me down the entrance gap to the school and escaped before the bell announcing the end of the first half-day had finished ringing.

I vividly remember participating in a camp fire in the headmaster's orchard with the Boy Scouts. I also remember participating in a route march with the cadet corps from the school to St John's Church. From the northern side of the church there is a fantastic view extending over to Hackleton's Cliff and beyond. When seen from the steeple of the church, it is a sight never to be forgotten.

My aunt's son, Dudley, was not so fortunate. He had entered the school a few weeks before I did, and when I told him my plan to get away on the first half-day, he replied, 'Not me, I'm staying to watch the First Eleven cricket.' He had become quite friendly with a number of senior white boys, perhaps because of his lighter skin colour. Dudley refused to leave the school compound on the first half-day; he ate his lunch and remained on the grounds and, when the cricket match started, he sat on the elevated wall to watch the game. This wall was near the headmaster's home and supported an aged tamarind tree. A white boy came by and said, 'You are a new boy, aren't you, what are you doing here?' Dudley answered, 'Can't you see I'm watching cricket?' The boy pushed him down the wall and, on the way down, his foot caught in the projecting roots of the tamarind tree and his leg broke. As a result, he had to spend the remainder of the term in bed.

I remember hearing Dudley's sister asking my sister one day what she proposed to do when she left school. She said, 'Because of my colour, I can get a job at Fogarty's, and what are you going to do?' Fogarty's was a big dry goods store at the top of Broad Street where the Norman Centre now stands. It was established by a parent firm in Guyana. The building was destroyed by fire in 1970.

Many years later, I was sitting in my office in the Government Headquarters one day when a gentleman strolled in and said to me: 'I am from Scotland and my name is Crawford and my search ends with you. I came here to check on my roots in Barbados. If ever you come to Scotland, come and see us. We are the Biscuit Company. It's easy to find us.' The story behind this was told to me years ago by an elder brother of my father called Lemuel whom I visited in Montreal. As I recall it, he related that his grandfather came from Scotland, and he was a doctor in the British Regiment stationed in Barbados. When the Regiment was disbanded, he decided to live in Barbados, acquired some land and built a house, right under the carving of the lion at Gun Hill. He was never married but he had several children with his black housekeeper. One of my father's sisters, called Maude, who died in New York some years ago, had hair which flowed to the middle of her back.

Before I went to Combermere, my family had moved from my mother's house in St Lawrence to 'Hillston', the house which my father had built about half a mile eastwards along the same main road. The contractor was Mr J.T.C. Ramsay, who himself became a member of the House of Assembly for a short while in the 1940s and created history in Barbados by entering the Chamber on his first appearance in a pair of overalls, to indicate his representation of the working classes.[3] This was reminiscent of Keir Hardie who did the same thing when he first entered the British House of Commons. I remember my mother telling me that she indicated to Mr. Ramsay that she wanted the living room in the house separated from the dining room by an arch. She had a passion for arches, which I inherited. Mr Ramsay gave her no end of trouble before he agreed to erect this arch.

My father was in those days chief engineer in charge of the rolling stock of the British Union Oil Company Ltd. that was then prospecting for oil in Barbados. He used to ride a bicycle to the headquarters of the Oil company at the Garrison and back everyday. There were not many cars in those days. Indeed, my father could stay inside the house, hear a car passing on the road, and tell whose car it was. When the prospecting operation for oil was reduced, the Director and my father were discharged. He then had a short contract with the Central Road Board when he and an English engineer, a Mr. Toogood, built the Pine road. To this day it remains among the most durable roads in Barbados. He then took charge of the City Garage owned by a Mr. James Inniss who went to America for some period of time, leaving my father and his secretary in charge of the business. By this time, my parents had other children, and my father was tired of riding his bicycle everyday. Because the other children might soon be going to school in St Michael, he decided to sell the house and move to St Michael. We moved to a comfortable two-story building at the corner of Beckwith Street, a block from Bay Street. My mother and the rest of the family did not like that house at all. My mother always preferred to live out of town so, when nearly all the children were finished school, we moved back to the old family house in St Lawrence, which had been rented in the meantime, and which, with some additions, suited us comfortably.

I remember a family who lived not far from our house in Beckwith Street; it was the Hoyos family. When I was a little over twelve, Mrs. Hoyos brought her son, Fabriciano, and asked me if I would be willing to give him lessons in Latin and French because she wanted him to sit for an exhibition to attend Harrison College. He was two years younger than I was. I gave him the lessons, and he won the exhibition. He later became Sir Fabriciano Hoyos, the biographer of the late Grantley Adams. Indeed, Grantley's brother is married to Fabriciano's sister, Isabella. As for myself, at the age of 14, I went on to win the Certificate of the Junior Examination set by the Oxford and Cambridge Joint Board. The following year I sat the senior examination but did not gain the certificate because I failed in mathematics and geography. I left Combermere at the age of 16, and my first action was to send an application to the Civil Service. I felt sure I could get in with my Junior Cambridge Certificate. I knew many boys who had been selected for the Service without it. When I was called up at the age of 16, I was told that I had the qualification and that I would be called up if I applied the following year. There were several people older than myself, without the qualification, whom they wanted to accom-modate. I never applied again. One reason was that while my friends in the Civil Service were being paid $20 a month, I was offered the job to act as cashier for a wholesale grocery in Roebuck Street which was then the island's main distribution centre for food. This was to lead to far more profitable prospects in the future.

Notes

1   Wynter Crawford was born on August 29, 1910.
2   There was at least one other 'coloured' teacher at the school during the 1920s. He was V.B. 'Bull' Williams, appointed in 1919, who taught at the school for over forty years.
3   J.T.C. Ramsay was a founder member of the Democratic League in 1924. He eventually represented the parish of St Peter in the House of Assembly from 1942 to 1945 as a member of the Progressive League (renamed the Barbados Labour Party).

Working In The Islands

By the time that temporary job ended, my family was offered the opportunity to spend time at the seaside at a house in Worthing which belonged to my mother's sister, Constance King. So far as I remember, either that or the place adjacent to it was taken over by the telephone company for a branch exchange. In those days, Worthing was not a residential area. From Skeete Hill to the road leading to St Lawrence Church, there were what are known as 'bay-houses', and people who could afford it rented these houses during the vacation period to take their children to the seaside. This was similar to the practice in Worthing, England, I presume. Today the area is both residential and commercial. My aunt would rent her house to quite a number of people from Guyana and Trinidad and Tobago.

When my aunt told my mother to bring the children and come up for a vacation, my mother in turn invited another friend of hers, a Mrs Gibbons and her family. One of the Gibbons' boys, Sam Gibbons, was later appointed manager of the airport. My mother, Mrs Gibbons and the two families were enjoying their vacation at the bay-house when the eldest girl, Gwen, who was working in the city, came home to say she was not feeling well and did not think she was going to work the next day. Mrs Gibbons asked my mother if she would allow me to go down and work for Gwen until she was fit to return to work. She was cashier and assistant manager of a dry goods store in Swan Street belonging to Mr and Mrs Hope. Mrs Hope used to manage the store when she finished her duties at her Bank Hall home. My mother said I was not working and wanted something to do and would be happy to go and do it for Gwen. So the next morning I went to the store in Swan Street to Mr Hope whose clothing business was adjacent to that of Mrs Hope. He first asked me if I could make out customs warrants. I said I could, and he asked if I could take dictation in shorthand. I said I had done dictation and transcription at 80 and 120 words a minute at the Oxford and Cambridge examinations. Shortly after beginning to dictate a letter, he said to me, 'Rather than dictate the letter, I'll tell you what I want written. I have a shipment of goods from England on a 90-day sight draft. The draft will be due shortly, and I want an extension. I want you to draft a letter to be sent to the firm in Huddersfield, England requesting them to ask the bank to be kind enough to extend the due date of the draft by another 30 days.' So I drafted a letter which he said was quite satisfactory. He told me to come to work the next week and I did.

In those days Broad Street and Swan Street comprised the main shopping centres of Bridgetown in an entirely different form from what they are now. There were no malls or boutiques. Broad Street boasted shopping houses like Fogarty's, Hope Ross, Whitfields, C.F. Harrison, while Swan Street boasted almost comparable houses like Goodridge, A.E. Taylor, Lashley, N.E. Wilson, Grannum and a number of first class jewellery stores like Ashby's, Brown and Co., Holder Brothers, and Nicholls.

Broad Street, Bridgetown

Gwen Gibbons never returned to the store. She got married some months later to Mr Walter Batson, a customs clerk in Roebuck Street. Some of her children now operate the Bits Travel Agency in Grenada, St Lucia and Barbados. One of her sisters married the late Mr Horace Hoyte, founder of Hoyte's Travel Services. Their son, Harold Hoyte, is the outstanding and internationally acclaimed editor of Barbados' biggest newspaper, the *Sunday Sun* and the *Nation* and the Managing Director of The Nation Publishing Company. To add to his distinguished career, Mr Hoyte was invited in 1992 to spend one year in Jamaica as editorial consultant to the *Gleaner*, the oldest newspaper in the West Indies.

I remained with Mr Hope for nearly a year, until the demands of Mrs Hope's increasing family gave her little time to attend to the business. Her husband's clothing business made suits for the middle and upper classes in Barbados and other West Indian islands, from Grenada to St Thomas and St Croix in the Virgin Islands. His firm and that of C.B. Rice and Co., an English-operated enterprise, stocked shirts, ties and considerable quantities of the best-made cloth for men's suits.

A customer would come in, choose the cloth, and the suit would be made and sent to his home in Barbados or to any of the other islands. Both these firms employed travelling salesmen who carried samples to clients in other islands and took their orders for samples of woollens, tweeds and serges, linens, doeskin and flannels, stocked from the most exclusive mills in England. They competed with one another for the patronage of the gentry in the smaller islands in the northern and southern Caribbean.

When I was invited to New York in 1938 by the West Indian Defence Committee, it was Mr. Hope who supplied me with the appropriate clothes. By that time he had set up a business in Martinique where English woollens were in great demand. From his stock of English vicuñas, he made me some clothes consisting of a morning coat, an evening coat with tails, a dress jacket and a tuxedo which could double as a morning coat as it carried no silk on the lapels. It is now fifty-three years since that time, and those clothes are in perfect condition. Indeed, less than a year ago, Mrs Enid Lynch, the retired headmistress and former member of the Legislative Council and her husband were staging a play in which these garments were required. I loaned them the clothes and they were amazed at their condition.

They were other well established firms in the city such as Clairmonte and Co. operated by Mr Ambrose Clairmonte, whose brother was Income Tax Commissioner. There was Mr P.T. O'Neale, the brother of the well known Dr Duncan O'Neale; there was Mr Stanley Heath who, at his father's death, had joined C.B. Rice and Co. together with another partner,

Mr Allan, from England. At this time (1927), Mr Hope had a travelling salesman called Mr Gooding who was about to retire. The job was taken over by Hope's nephew, Mr Livingstone Goring, who made a trip to Grenada and died soon afterwards. Mr Hope asked if I would take over as travelling salesman. I was delighted with the prospect of seeing all the islands and immediately replied that I would.

I travelled through the islands for about two years or more, booking orders from the samples I carried, and thoroughly enjoyed it. In the U.S. Virgin Islands of St Thomas and St Croix, the firm had a permanent agent, Mr Robert Fredericks; he was a Grenadian living there and was a member of the Legislative Council in St Croix. When I went to St Croix I stayed at his home, and he turned over any orders he had to me and then recanvassed for new orders.

Shipping vessels, battleships and tourist liners all looked forward to stopping in Barbados to shop for high quality material. I remember walking along the waterfront one day and seeing some naval officers arguing with a boatman or, rather, trying to tell the boatman what they wanted. They were speaking Spanish. I had taken both French and Spanish in my Junior Oxford and Cambridge Examination, so I intervened and found out that they wanted to know where they could get the best men's clothing. Mr Hope had by then transferred his business to Martinique, so I introduced the three officers to C.B. Rice and Co. and Mr Rice immediately offered to give me a commission on the sales made from the ship. I met most of the other officers at the business place and acted as interpreter. I received ten per cent on their orders, and was offered a job with the firm.

I decided I had done enough travelling, so I left the clothing industry. In the meantime, my father, who was a motor and marine engineer, had been recommended by Sir Harold Austin of Gardiner Austin and Co. to take up a contract in Grenada where they were extending the light and power services. He was not fussy about going, but I told him that I knew Grenada because I had spent some time there, and that I would go with him while he familiarized himself with the place. So we went to Grenada and I stayed for a month with him. On my way home, I decided to see some friends in St Vincent. While there, I was offered a job operating a cinema belonging to a Mr DeFreitas. I stayed for over six months, until he was notified that he would no longer be able to get silent movies. The company in the USA was introducing 'talkies'. Mr DeFreitas operated a number of businesses in St Vincent, including groceries and dry goods shops, and he said he could not afford at that time to invest in 'talkie' equipment. I then decided to return to Barbados and find employment.

I recall an amusing incident while I was in St Vincent. Some friends of mine from Trinidad were on vacation at a seaside place called Edinboro. The eldest boy, Elton, and I had become good friends. The family had an uncle, Mr Dyer, who lived in St Vincent. The government was taking a census of the population, and Mr Dyer was asked to supervise the entire operation. He called in Elton one day and told him that there was a village in the mountains with what were known as 'Bajan bacras'. This village, known as Dorsetshire, is similar to the village Mount Moritz in Grenada which is inhabited solely by the same ethnic group.[1] Mr Dyer told Elton that he had to have the census rechecked for that entire village because there were many errors, and asked him to undertake the job.

The only way to reach the village was on horseback, and Elton had very little experience with horseback riding. He said the only way he would undertake it was if Wynter Crawford was sent to assist him. He approached me, and I said that it would be a good exercise and that we should try it together because of my earlier experience with horseback riding. We hired two horses from a Mr Gonsalves in Kingstown and started to ride up the mountain path, a very narrow ledge up a steep mountain. As we approached the village along a winding path, we regretted having undertaken the task because it was obviously dangerous. Had the horses slipped, we would have been pitched thousands of feet below. As soon as we got to the top of the mountain, we dismounted. The horses started to neigh loudly, turned around and pranced down the hill. We watched them going downhill when the contour of the hillside permitted us to see them. We were not disturbed by their departure because it would have been even more dangerous to ride them down the steep incline. We checked the census as fast as we could, corrected the errors that had been made, and started to walk down the hillside. We got down to the bottom very late in the evening and went to Mr Gonsalves to tell him what had happened. He said we were not to worry because the horses had come straight back home.

My earlier experiences with horseback riding were on the beach near Dover. My aunt's husband, whom I have mentioned earlier, lived next door to us in St Lawrence. I mentioned that my aunt kept a horse and double buggy. On Sunday mornings, the groom used to take this horse to the beach near Dover to give it exercise and a sea bath. There was a friend living not far from there, named Garnes, who kept a horse and buggy for taking children to school. The two horses were taken to the beach on Sunday mornings and my cousin Dudley and I used to ride these horses up and down. One Sunday morning, Mr Garnes' son, Hugh, was

A Youthful Wynter Crawford

riding his father's horse and I got a long piece of grass and tickled the horse under the tail. Garnes saw me coming and I held the reins when the horse reared, but it did not throw him off. I forgot about the incident and, some Sundays later, while I was riding, Garnes hid behind some bush and, after I had passed, came out with a long piece of stick to tickle my horse under the tail. The horse reared and threw me into the sea.

On my return to Barbados from St Vincent, I was considering what should be the next step to take by way of employment when I was approached by a friend, Carlton Holder. He was the youngest of three brothers who ran a very successful and popular jewellery and later pawn-broking business in Swan Street. He said that the firm was doing well but he wanted to try his luck abroad for a short while. So he put a proposition to me. He said, 'You have been travelling within the region for a few years now and you know all the gentry in these islands who order clothes from Barbados. What do you think of the idea of taking about three journeymen tailors from Barbados to establish a custom clothing business in one of the islands? You know the sources of most of the best woollens, "palm beaches", white and coloured linens imported into Barbados by Hope and Rice from England. We will order cloth and get these tailors to supply suits to your clients in the islands.' I thought about it and said, 'Well, Antigua is the seat of government of the Leeward Islands.' As a matter of fact, the Governor along with other federal officials lived there. We decided to carry three experienced workmen to Antigua: Mr Lorde, Mr Rawlins and Mr Chandler. We took a small amount of material with us and we set up business in the main business street of St John's, Antigua a few months before my twenty-first birthday, which I celebrated in Antigua. Captain Whitty, who was private secretary to the Governor of Antigua, was one of the first customers to come in and order half a dozen suits of white linen. As far as I remember, he was very pleased with the suits when he received them.

We remained in Antigua for a few months and business was not bad. However, Carlton Holder's brothers were adding a pawn-broking

department to their jewellery store and asked Carlton to return to
Barbados to assist them with it. He agreed to go back home. So I
decided to close down the business place. Two of the tailors returned
to Barbados but Mr Lorde remained in Antigua.

Notes

1   Both settlements were a consequence of sponsored poor white immigration
    from Barbados. The Dorsetshire settlement may have been established in 1858
    while the Mount Moritz settlement was started around 1875.

CHAPTER 3

The Barbadian Social Scene

The background against which I grew up and came to political maturity was limited in cultural stimulation and always overshadowed by colour prejudice. There was not much in the way of literary and educational activity on a community basis in Barbados. There was Weymouth Club which was a debating society; it seemed to have developed out of the Moravian Sunday School. The Hewitts and the Hayneses and some others used to meet and practise debating and hold mock trials. I heard that Frank Walcott was associated with Weymouth.

Another group was the Riverside Club. They held their meetings in the old railway building overlooking the Constitution River. They were associated with the Goodwill League which was founded by John Beckles who ran a laundry business and dye-works and was a noted social worker in his time. One of the main functions of the Goodwill League was to raise funds for the baby crèche which was one of the earliest day-crèches for the children of poor working mothers. Winnie Ward, later Lady Ward, wife of Erskine Ward, was one of the leaders. They practised a little debating and held small functions like concerts and dances, but their main interest was in social welfare. Some of the members, like Madame Ifill and May Hall, broke away and formed their own welfare organizations. They did not have any great significance in the society except that they were pioneers in social welfare work.

The Forum was a small literary group which published the *Forum* magazine. That's all. It was probably edited by Gordon Bell. I know H.A. Vaughan, J.C. Hope and Gladstone Holder were associated with it. There are copies of the magazine around. I know the Museum and Archives have some of them. They would probably have the names of the Committee. But they were mainly concerned with the publication of the *Forum*. I have no recollection that they involved themselves with politics or social welfare or anything like that.

Clennell Wickham had started a magazine too. After he lost the *Herald*, before he went to Grenada, he started a publication called the *Outlook*. It was well written, of course, in true Wickham style. It had some very good articles, but I doubt that he had more than a couple of issues because he could not get advertisers to support it. It was the same with the *Barbados Observer*. For all the years of publication we never had an advertisement from DaCosta, as far as I know. We used to have Cave Shepherd and Harrison, but most of the big firms would never advertise at all because of the policies we had. Similarly with the *Herald*; there were two *Heralds*. After Wickham's *Herald* closed down, a small committee comprising 'Chrissie' Brathwaite, J.A. Martineau and Charlie Elder got together and tried to revive it. Years later, when I was in New York looking for printing equipment, a man called Grannum told me that 'Chrissie' Brathwaite had come to New York looking for printing equipment. He got a second-hand press and some printing material which he sent to Barbados. That is how the new *Herald* was started.

Charlie Elder used to write the leading articles, but it never had the policies of the old *Herald*. When I started the *Observer*, the new *Herald* was already being published. So there were altogether six newspapers: the *Advocate*, the *Herald*, the *Recorder*, the *Times* and the *Weekly Illustrated* as well as my own newspaper. When the war started, two journalists were invited to London from every territory in the West Indies by the British Government to witness the war effort at first hand. I was not interested at all in going.

I had just started the *Observer* and I was not going to leave it. They selected Louis Gale from the *Advocate*, Ian Gale's father, and Fred Cole who had just started the *Recorder*; Harold Wilson from Antigua, and quite a few others went up. It was a perilous undertaking. They travelled by ship on seas infested with submarines and, in crossing the Atlantic, they had to sleep with all their clothes on. But when they got to Bermuda, Gale and Cole (whom you would probably call mulattoes) were not accepted in the big hotels in Bermuda. They had to go to a hotel used by coloured people. It caused a furore there.

✳ INCORRECT — VALANCE GALE WAS THE FOUNDER OF THE ADVOCATE AND HE FATHER OF IAN AND TREVOR GALE.

Colour prejudice was rampant here in Barbados too. I tried on several occasions to do something about it. Before the coalition (in 1946), I had tabled a report on the floor of the House calling on the Government to introduce legislation to compel business houses in Bridgetown and the banks and other large-scale employers to employ a certain percentage of non-white labour because, if you were coloured, you could not get a job in a bank. You could not go into DaCosta's office upstairs or Brydens or Barbados Mutual and find a coloured person.

I wrote an editorial in the *Observer* asking people not to buy Singer sewing machines because only the porter at Singer was black. We had a cigarette called 'Trumpeter' which was made in a factory down by what is now the Deep Water Harbour and it was smoked exclusively by the lower and working classes but no black girl could work in there making those cigarettes or rolling the tobacco or anything. This was done mostly by hand in those days. The man in charge was a white man, from the southern states of America, who built that house at the corner of Worthing View where Barclays Bank now has a branch. So I walked in there one day and told him I wanted to discuss a matter with him. He said, 'Yes, Mr. Crawford, what can I do for you?' I was editor of the *Observer* at the time. I said, 'Look, I've come to discuss with you a little matter which I think deserves attention – your factory here – I can see all the girls working. Your cigarettes are bought by the working classes in Barbados, by the man on the street – all black people – and you do not have a single black girl working here.' So he ordered me out. He said, 'Mr Crawford, get out before I put you out of my office. You cannot come in here and tell me how to run my place.' I said, 'When I have finished with you in the *Observer*, you will not sell a cigarette in Barbados!'

A coloured person could not go to the Aquatic Club. It even had its own cinema, and the coloured people were not allowed to go there. They sent me tickets a couple of times purely as a newspaper editor and I never bothered with them at all. A similar ban existed at clubs like the Bridgetown Club, the Savannah Club, and the Yacht Club. There used to be, every Old Year's night, a costume dance at the Marine Hotel. Coloured people were not allowed to go into it at all. There were two other dances on Old Year's night, one at Empire Cricket Club and the other at Spartan Cricket Club where coloured people used to go. But, if you went up by the Marine, you would see the place packed with cars, with light-skinned people sitting down on top of the motor car bonnets and that kind of thing, watching the costumes go in. They could not go in themselves. I know a coloured chap (he is still living now) who went in a costume with his wife one night and they told her she could go in but he could not. She went in and left him outside.

The Hotel Royal was built by a man called A.E. Taylor. He would say that he was white. He had a store in Swan Street. He used to advertise in my newspaper. He said to me, 'We are opening the Hotel Royal on Friday night and I have arranged for someone to take a photograph and put it in the newspaper.' I was going through the Public Buildings yard the same morning and Erskine Ward stopped me and said, 'I just told off A.E. Taylor.' I said, 'What happened?' He said, 'You know his new hotel? He sent me an invitation for the opening, but somebody told me that he said that he does not want any coloured people or black people around there, but there were some he would have to invite because of the positions they occupied in the country.' He had to invite the Registrar, Erskine Ward, Frank Holder, and a few more. So Erskine said to me, 'I told Taylor, "I got an invitation but I am not coming. I am the same black man as you." 'What did Taylor say?' I asked. 'He could not say anything. He just walked off.'

Barbados was perhaps the only country in the entire West Indies that preserved the rigid racial discrimination after emancipation because so many whites remained and controlled the land and commercial enterprises. Take for instance Grenada or Dominica or St Lucia; in Grenada I doubt if there are six white families. I was in Dominica once for six months, and the whites could not have a public dance unless they invited the coloured people. They were not enough. It was easier for a coloured person to go and play tennis in the white tennis club than the reverse. Personally, I would admit that, despite the racial discrimination and the social conditions which it created, in certain fields and in technological advance the whites have made a contribution to the country. There is a possibility that much of the superiority which Barbados has over most of the other islands is due to the combination of people of all colours who have contributed to the

Hotel Royal, 1943

progress of the country. We have nothing to be ashamed of when we compare ourselves to some of the islands which are bigger in population. I would say that, by and large, colour discrimination was more rampant in Barbados than possibly in any other island in the West Indies.

The coloured people at one time formed the *coloured* Aquatic Club at Worthing, and we used to go there and dance; and on Sunday mornings we would go there and have drinks and bathe in the sea. The first secretary was a man called Arthur McKenzie. He was not exactly suited to be the head, so the club did not last too long. After that, we had a small club behind Talma's house at Rockley. We used to go there on Friday and Saturday nights and some nights during the week and dance. Most people, however, confined their parties to their homes because there were not many hotels and they were not welcome in the big hotels. There were only the Marine and Taylor's Royal; anybody could go to Taylor's Royal. In spite of his attempt to discriminate at the opening ceremony, the coloured people started going in there as they liked, right from the beginning. As a matter of fact, we had a small party there for Alexander Bustamante of Jamaica until 3:00 a.m. He

Bustamante 3ʳᵈ from right on arrival at Seawell Airport in Barbados on 6 May 1951 with Wynter Crawford at centre

was in Barbados staying at the Marine. There were no hotels on the West Coast then. The very first hotel on the West Coast was started by a man from Canada called Martin Griffith. I was in Canada and he called me and told me that he was coming down here to start a hotel. After the winter season, he used to close it down and spend the remainder of the year living in the south of France. In Christ Church, we had only Taylor's, the Marine, Marson's place – Ocean View – and the Windsor which was built by a man called Parravacino, who was the Italian Consul. There was also the Crane, a very old hotel, and Sam Lord's Castle owned by the Goddards. There was also Powell Spring at Bathsheba and, after a while, Edgewater and Atlantis.

The Young Journalist

I had been studying journalism on my own and, after we closed the business in Antigua, I toyed with the idea of starting a newspaper there. Antigua had a newspaper called the *Magnet*, run by a Barbadian, Mr Harold Wilson. He was getting on in age and the publication reflected this decline. His was the only newspaper in the island, whereas most of the other islands had two. Dominica had the *Chronicle* and the *Tribune*; St Kitts had the *Bulletin* and the *Union Messenger*; St Lucia had the *Voice* and the *Crusader*; and Montserrat had no paper at all.

To get back to starting a newspaper: I was toying with the idea and I thought advertisers would be glad. Then I figured that, if I started it, it might interfere with Mr Wilson's income and, apart from the fact that he was getting on in age, he was a Barbadian. I did not want to offer him competition. So I then decided to publish a monthly magazine, the *Leeward Islands Monthly Review*. The first edition, printed and published, had quite a few advertisements and a few good articles, one of which was written by the Reverend J.E. Levo, a prominent Anglican priest, outlining some of the history of the Leewards. I employed a printer who apparently thought that he should be publishing the magazine himself, and he imposed terms which made it impossible for me to get a second edition out utilizing his services. So I ordered a Kelsey printing outfit, a small hand-press and Linotype machine, and other equipment from America. I employed an assistant, and we published the second edition ourselves from an empty room in the house where I lived.

After publishing the second edition in Antigua, I got an offer of a job to act as editor of the *Tribune* in Dominica for six months while the nominal editor, Dr P.C. Christian, a prominent dentist, was on vacation. The mast-head bore the name of Dr Christian as editor but the editor was really Mr C.E.A. Rawle, a lawyer and member of the Legislative Council. He did not realise his full ambition to become Chief Justice but he later became Attorney-General. My understanding was that the paper was jointly owned by Mr Rawle and the Hon A.C. Shillingford, the wealthiest planter/merchant in Dominica. He and his brother owned several estates and drug stores, dry goods stores, grocery stores, you name it. I really liked Dominica and spent six months there. The people were predominately Roman Catholic and were very hospitable.

I remember an incident there which stuck in my mind for years. One afternoon, a young lady came into the newspaper office. Her name was Medora Gehben, and she said she was from Hollywood and had been sent by the film producers, Pathé Gazette, to do some work among the Caribs in Dominica. Pathé Gazette produced shorts or documentaries which were sold to theatres all over the world to be shown before the regular picture started. Miss Gehben wanted to know if I could assist her as to what steps she should take, first, to get among the Caribs, and then spend some time on the reservation. I told her I would be happy to do anything I could, but I could not spend too much time with her because I was going to cover a football match. She said, 'Football match! I have never seen one, could you take me along to see it?' I said, 'I have a motorcycle and can carry only a pillion rider at the back and you might not like it.' She said, 'No, I'd love it.' Miss Gehben found the game both interesting and entertaining.

At the end of the match, I invited her to the Roseau Club for a Dominica rum punch. This was a club in the city where the *jeunesse dorée* of Dominica spent time, playing tennis, having a few rum punches and general chit-chat after work on afternoons. The moment I entered with her I noticed the atmosphere seemed to chill; it was not the way I was normally greeted. I had introduced her to a few people when, to my surprise, the secretary of the club called me aside. Her name was Josephine Roberts, and I knew her before going to Dominica. She and her sister had been to school in Barbados at Queens College as young girls and had boarded with a friend of my mother's. She said, 'Wynter, you are a temporary member of the club and we're happy to have you, and you are always welcome, but you should never bring a white woman here unless you ask permission first.' I said, 'What?' She said, 'We are very strict about this; if you want to bring a white person here, you first have to get the permission of the club; white people are not allowed to walk in here as they like.' She said, 'It is easier for one of us to go to the white club next door than for a white person to come into the "Roseau". They can't hold a public dance or reception unless they invite us, and we have strict rules about how they participate in our social activities. It is not like Barbados where it is just the opposite.' I was somewhat embarrassed by the almost frigid welcome they gave to Miss Gehben at the "Roseau".

Apparently, after emancipation most of the whites left so, as in Grenada, most of the estates and lands in Dominica are owned by the black people. The government owned a lot of Crown lands too. The story of Medora Gebhen illustrates the difference between what went on in Barbados with the Bridgetown Club, the Savannah Club, and the Yacht Club and what went on in the other islands.

The six months as acting editor of the *Tribune* was a great experience. The editor, Mr Rawle, gave me no end of trouble. Sometimes I would write an editorial which I thought was fair but he wanted the government praised; at other times he wanted the government attacked. The other owner of the newspaper, the Hon. A.C. Shillingford, gave me no trouble at all.

Dominica is a fascinating country, with beautiful rivers and waterfalls. Most of the coloured gentry had plantations in the country where they spent weekends in the plantation houses with their mistresses while their wives were in the city. I used to go to a place called the Riviere Claire Doreqe which was owned by the Simon family. It was near the Doreé Estate owned by the Shillingfords. The plantation next door was also owned by people I knew. I lived at a place that was run by the widow of a Barbadian barrister. On Sundays the place was crowded with ladies who came from church.

Land was very cheap; you could buy Crown land at two shillings (48 cents) an acre, but then you would have to clear it of trees and forests. Most people had a little garden growing potatoes, yams and cassava. I remember a schooner captain telling me one day, 'You know, I brought a load of cargo to Barbados and I offered the men a price to unload it, and they said it was too low. I said, 'Alright, let it stay.' They hung around for a while and then they came back to unload the cargo at my price. But in Dominica when I offer a price, they refuse my offer. At lunchtime, they go home and eat, they come back and sit around and hold up my ship until I have to pay charges. Eventually, I have to pay them what they want because they are never hungry. They reap potatoes and yams and other vegetables from their plots of land and catch fish in the river. Every man has a little garden somewhere where he grows vegetables and his own foodstuff.'

Most of the land in Dominica was owned by coloured people. Most of the estates had a river running through them as well as waterfalls. We enjoyed going to the waterfalls to bathe in the afternoon. I remember an incident connected with the estate next door that belonged to a friend of the Shillingfords. Sometimes we would go over there to bathe under their waterfall. One afternoon we went just in time to see an interesting scene taking place. There was a half-Carib girl with apparently her mother and two well-known brothers having an altercation. The girl's mother was a Carib and the girl was insisting that she be allowed to accept the invitation from one of the brothers who wanted to take her into the city to set her up in an establishment. The mother was equally adamant that she should not go and was exclaiming, 'Mon Dieu! Mon Dieu! any man except that man!' But the girl insisted that she was going with him. As she insisted, the mother shouted, 'You cannot go with that man, any man but that man; that man is your father!' Unfortunately, the girl had already slept with him the night before.

Just as I was scheduled to leave Dominica, I got an invitation from the Montserrat Cotton Growers Association to visit Montserrat to consider the possibility of starting a newspaper there. Montserrat had no newspaper at all. I did not think I would be interested in living there but I accepted the invitation. I stayed with a Miss Osbourne who had a guest house. On a more recent visit there, I stayed with her nephew who owned the best hotel in Montserrat, the "Vue Pointe", commanding a beautiful view on a hill overlooking the sea. My only objection was that the sand was black or nearly black. Anyhow, I went and toured the city to survey the place, and decided I could not possibly live there. The place was too small, and there was not any prospect of making a living with a newspaper where the population is so small. They claim the Montserrat population in New York is bigger than the ten or twelve thousand people actually in Montserrat.

When I was there, I experienced an earthquake. I awoke to find my clothes falling on the floor and the dressing table shaking. I realized that this must be an earthquake and I went back to sleep. When I went into the city next morning, there was considerable damage. All the churches were down with the exception of the Salvation Army building and, for sometime after that, the Catholics, Anglicans and Methodists all had to share the Salvation Army building to hold their services. This prompted Clennell Wickham, an outstanding Barbadian journalist, to observe in an article in the Herald newspaper that it took an earthquake to unite the churches in Montserrat! I was in Montserrat for nearly a week or so when a lawyer, Mr J.M.R. Meade, approached me and asked me if I wrote shorthand. He said, 'Could you report the court proceedings of a murder case for me? I have been appointed to defend a woman charged with the murder of her husband's son, and the case is going to drag on for some time because I know the judge and what to expect from him. I have arranged your accommodation and so on.' I accepted the offer. We went to the court on the first day of the case. The judge was an Englishman, Mr Berlyn, and prosecuting for the crown was a Mr Richards, Crown Attorney from St Lucia; his assistant chief clerk was Mr Auguste Pinard who afterwards became a Permanent Secretary to Errol Barrow in Barbados.

This was probably the most amusing incident I have ever seen in all my life. The woman was accused of poisoning her husband's son with a banana in which she had inserted some seeds from a plant called the *datura stramonium* (a species of Deadly Nightshade). The boy ate the banana, vomited and died. A dog ate the vomit and also died. She was charged with the murder of the boy. The government apparently gave the defendant this lawyer, Mr Meade, to plead for her. The main evidence for the Crown was supplied by Mr Collins who was the government's bacteriologist and chemist in one other of the Leeward Islands.

It was a small court in the capital, Plymouth, and the judge sat on a raised dais along with Collins. There were two rows of seats below him on which Meade, Pinard, Crown Attorney Richards and myself were sitting. The case proceeded as long as it did because of the numerous adjournments every day. On the slightest pretext, the judge would order an adjournment of the Court, and he and the government's bacteriologist would retire to a room in the back for a short while and come back out again. Meade was probably a good lawyer, but he certainly was not cut out to be a criminal lawyer.

I read quite a few books during the trial. As a matter of fact, I came across one in a store in the city written by a woman called Vicky Vaughan. She had written *Grand Hotel*. It had some very purple passages in it and every time I saw a few I would hand the book to somebody and we would laugh and read this thing and amuse ourselves right under the judge in court. He did not pay us any mind at all. The trial proceeded and very often, when Meade was going to dismiss a prosecution witness, I would say, 'Oh no! Mr. Meade, call her back. Ask her so and so.' So he would ask her some more questions and I would tell him what to ask her, and the judge never said a word.

Anyhow, it came out during the proceedings that the accused was alleged to have given this poisoned banana to the boy while she was carrying a bucket of water on her head and, at this stage of the proceedings, the judge said to the Crown Attorney, 'Mr Richards, it is physically impossible for anybody to carry a bucket of water and at the same time hand a poisoned banana to a child.' The Crown Attorney said, 'Oh no, your Honour, it is quite common in the West Indies. I have seen people in the West Indies carrying buckets full of water on their heads without holding the bucket at all, with both hands at their sides and balancing the bucket.' 'Impossible! Impossible!' replied the judge, 'I would have to see it demonstrated in court. I have never seen it done and I am sure the jury has never seen it done. We will have a bucket of water brought into court and we will see if the defendant can do what you say. Court adjourned!' So he adjourned the court and later in the afternoon they brought in this bucket filled with water to give the woman and asked her to demonstrate in court for the jury to see whether she could walk any distance with the water balanced on her head without holding it. I said to Meade, 'Meade we are going to have some fun in here today, you know.' So the stupid woman went down to the bottom of the courtroom. She said first she could not carry the bucket unless she had a wad on her head. So the judge said, 'Mr Crown Attorney, I have never seen a wad and I am sure none of the jury has ever seen a wad. Court adjourned while you get a wad.' So they brought in this wad some time afterwards and the woman went down to the bottom of the court. She put the bucket of water on her head with the wad, and stupidly walked from the end of the courtroom up through the spectators to the edge of the platform where the jury and the judge were and never held the bucket at all. The judge said, 'Mr Crown Attorney, I can't believe it. It is not possible. Let her do it again!' As she went back to the end of the room to do this thing again and, I said, 'Meade, watch out now.' As she was coming back up, as soon as she got to the platform, she tripped and threw the bucket of water on the jury. A lot of them got their clothes wet. Berlyn adjourned the court immediately. Of course, she was found guilty and condemned. The day the judge was to pronounce the death sentence on her, the police orderly had to take up the black cap and put on his head since he could not put it on himself. Meade of course appealed the verdict. I do not know what happened to the appeal because I left the country.

I thought it was interesting to see the way things went on sometimes in these small places and the officials whom one had to encounter sometimes from the Colonial Office. I was not in Dominica when it occurred, but I was told that the same judge tried a case there in which a merchant, A.C. Shillingford, was suing a firm in America for money due to him for a shipment of bananas. The bananas arrived in a rotten condition and the consignee refused to pay and, of course, Shillingford's attorney argued that when the bananas left the port of Roseau they were in excellent condition. Berlyn asked the Crown Attorney how the bananas got from the shore to ship, because there was no deep water harbour. The Crown Attorney said, 'Oh, Your Honour, the bananas are trans-shipped by lighter from shore to ship.' Berlyn said, 'Mr Crown Attorney, I have never seen a lighter. What is a lighter? I am sure the jury have never seen a lighter. Have a lighter brought into court as an exhibit to show the jury what a lighter is and to demonstrate whether or not anything could have happened to the bananas while they were being transported from the shore to the ship. Court adjourned.' He adjourned as usual. This is the sort of thing that was going on in the Leeward Islands.

Berlyn must have been the Circuit Judge for the Leeward Islands at the time. I think I heard once that he was recalled. He could not have gone on longer after that Montserrat trial anyhow. He was a joke.

As a young man, my primary interest was the law. As a matter of fact, I went to Guadeloupe at one time because I was told that I could get across by boat from Pointe-à-Pitre to Bordeaux or Marseilles for sixty West Indian dollars. My intention was to go across in one of these boats and then go across to England and do some work and get through with my law. Twice I had intended doing law and each time I was frustrated. Unfortunately for me, when I went to Guadeloupe – this must have been somewhere around 1930–1932 – the boat took passengers across only during the summer months because they had no heating accommodation. Therefore I could not go.

When the war started I was preparing to go to England. Shortly after it ended, I started preparations to travel to England once again. I had a friend in England, Bennett Niles, doing law, and he sent me down the entrance papers for the Inns of Court. I went to J.B. Chenery who was Acting Chief Justice at the time and he and Hilton Vaughan signed the papers for me, but nothing came of it.

I was very interested in journalism as well. I was particularly interested in American journalists like Lincoln Steffens and the editor of the *American Mercury*, H.L. Mencken. But I did a lot of work on American journalists more so than on English ones, and I did a lot of reading and studying on the subject. I think that after a while I found it was my natural bent so I just stuck to it.

In the 1920s and 1930s only those who were fortunate enough to win the one Barbados scholarship per year, or those, like E.R.L. Ward and 'Jubie' Reece whose fathers could afford to send them to England to study, could become lawyers. It was customary for the aspiring lawyer on his return to enter politics for a short time, then get a government job, and work his way up from there.

In my time Allan Collymore, who became Attorney-General and then Chief Justice, had been in politics and from there he went to the Bench. Walter Reece followed the same pattern. He was in the House for St Lucy, then he became Attorney-General and, in fact, Mrs. Reece was reported to have been telling her maids that they would soon be calling her Lady Reece. Because of a clash with the Governor, he was never appointed Chief Justice. Keith Walcott was the same. He came back from World War I and entered politics for St James. Eventually he became Attorney-General and he would have been Chief Justice had it not been for a clash between himself and Sir Grattan Bushe, the Governor.[1] Erskine Ward was a very forthright advocate of the working class when he entered the House but the big planters asked his father if he would let him ruin them. He was eventually put on the bench as a magistrate and left politics.[2] Another example is Frank Holder. He entered the House for St Andrew, played the usual cards, became Solicitor-General and ended up on the judicial bench in British Guiana as Sir Frank Holder.

I remember one night going to a meeting in Kingstown, St Vincent and a man named Bryan Cox, a lawyer, was holding a meeting because he was trying to get into the Legislative Council. Even in St Vincent, his opponents were saying, 'Don't listen to Cox, he just wants to try to get a job.'

Grantley Adams himself would have walked the same road. Twice he applied for the post of Solicitor-General and failed. As editor of the *Agricultural Reporter*, he had served the Conservatives well by attacking Charles Duncan O'Neal, Clennell Wickham and people like B.L. Barrow, so he was very disappointed when he was rebuffed. However, I believe that when he saw the strength which the popular following gave to Clement Payne, he was motivated to turn to politics instead. In those days in politics, the only lawyer in Barbados who was not interested in and did not apply at some time for a government job was J.E.T. Brancker.

Even the ladies who were engaged in social welfare work got bitten by this extraordinary ambition to win British honours. I remember one lady, who was very interested in social welfare work, on hearing that one of her colleagues with an MBE had died, went around asking what would become of the MBE of the deceased and if could she get it. The men wanted to end up as British knights. As late as the 1960s, I was surprised when a young lawyer sitting beside me in the House said, 'Crawf, I don't care how the corn sells, I got to be a knight by forty.' At the Montego Bay Federation of the West Indies Conference, I met a chap called Courtenay who was a lawyer and the delegate from British Honduras (Belize), who afterwards became Sir Harrison Courtenay. He and I were sitting there chatting when a man came striding down towards us. Courtenay said, 'Crawf, do you know that chap?' I said, 'Yes. He is Garnet Gordon from St Lucia.' He said, 'My God! man, I bet you he is an OBE. Man he got a walk like an OBE.' Garnet did afterwards become Sir Garnet Gordon.

The West Indies owe a great deal to the example set by people like Norman Manley and Eric Williams who were in no way attracted by British titles or any such honours. Reports were that Manley had been offered a knighthood and that he had refused it because, when he was in the British armed forces before World War I, he could not obtain a commission because of his colour. Even Forbes Burnham in Guyana refused to allow one of his officials to accept a knighthood. I remember hearing Grantley Adams speaking at a meeting here in Barbados after the Federation broke up. What he said about his knighthood and the authority he attached to it was shocking. One could not believe that that kind of thing meant so much to him.

It was so much the pattern to move from politics to a government job that it even affected me. Once when I had an outstanding verbal clash with Sir Laurie Pile's son (Douglas Pile), who was Speaker of the House, the very next morning the manager of the Gas Company, an Englishman called Brown, walked into my office and told me he had been sent by both the Attorney-General and the Speaker of the House to know if I would be interested in a job. So I said, 'A job, Mr. Brown? What are you talking about?' He said, 'Look here, Mr. Crawford, you know you all want jobs.' Now for the first time they were going to appoint a Labour Commissioner. They had brought in a man called Guy Perrin, the first Labour Commissioner of Barbados. Brown said to me, 'There is no provision yet for an assistant to Perrin, but if you would take the job as his assistant, we would give it to you at the same salary as a Police Magistrate, $200 per month (that was the salary of a Police Magistrate then). When Perrin's contract expires you will become the Labour Commissioner at a salary of $300 per month.' I told him he was very kind but I was not interested in any job. So he walked out and went and reported to those who had sent him. That afternoon, the Clerk of the House himself, a solicitor, Lee Sergeant, called me and said, 'I'd like to see you about a little matter.' He said, 'I know your father and I know you, don't make yourself a fool; look at me, I was the big man in the Christ Church Vestry for years, I was the churchwarden for years, I was member of the House, look at me. Now I got to take a job in the Government – Clerk of the House. Take the job man. Don't be stupid. If you take that job, you will probably end up as Governor of Barbados one of these days.' The words came back to my mind when, later in Trinidad, Solomon Hochoy, who had been Labour Commissioner there, was appointed Governor by Eric Williams when Trinidad and Tobago became independent. Anyway, I told Sergeant that I was very sorry but I was not interested in the job at all, because I was doing pretty well on my own. Within about two weeks, I went to a party one night at the Marine Hotel and the Deputy Director of Agriculture, Mackintosh, came up to me and said, 'Mr. Crawford, I hear you playing the fool. You know all of you want jobs. What are you playing at? Why are you playing about?' I was getting a bit annoyed. So his wife came and said to me, 'Mr Crawford, don't take him too seriously. He is a bit under the weather.' And she took him away.

I would not have returned to Barbados when I did were it not for the fact that my father (who had other children to support) had begun to lose his sight. I was in Montserrat when my mother wrote and told me that my father's sight was failing, so I decided to return to Barbados. I had bought a small amount of printing equipment in Dominica from a man called Emmanuel. He had a small printing plant which I had purchased and taken to Montserrat with me. I left it there while I came back here to see my father and then went back to Montserrat for it. I then returned to Barbados and decided to start the *Observer* at the age of twenty-four. That was in 1934.

After the war started, I published a small daily catalogue with only war news which was called the *Daily News*. It was not too long, or the effort would have killed me. You could not get any equipment. I had only one Linotype Machine and I had to be working day and night, so I went down to Bathsheba for a weekend. While there on the Saturday, my mother telephoned and said that the Governor, Sir Grattan Bushe, wanted to see me immediately. I told the ADC that I would see the Governor on Monday when I came down. At that time there were four newspaper editors – Louis Gale from the *Advocate*, Fred Cole from the *Recorder*, Charlie Elder from the *Herald*, and myself from the *Barbados Observer*. Every Thursday morning, we had to go to Government House for a press conference to discuss the war and related matters. There was also a press censor, an Englishman called J. Walker Paton who was supposed to examine the newspapers before they were put on the street, but he never bothered us at all. He had an office at the corner of Roebuck Street in a building owned by Johnson & Redman. I do not know what happened between him and Hugh Springer, but Hugh Springer came in to the House of Assembly one day and blasted him in a speech. I think Paton was a bit of an alcoholic too, because Hugh said, among other things, that it was not by accident that his office was upstairs 'J & R', which was a very famous Barbados rum.

On Monday morning, I went to the ADC's office, and he said, 'Mr Crawford, have a seat. I want to talk to you. To begin with, I do not know where you get your war news from, but it is days ahead of the *Advocate* which has it two or three days after you. And you are always accurate. Britain and her allies have cracked the Axis code and we now know that Rommel's aim is to seize Dakar. Now, if Dakar falls, and we can't stop it, and Rommel also takes Egypt, we are finished. The Germans plan to come straight down through the West Indies to the Panama Canal, so we will be in the war. We would be in the line of defence. You have published a report about the Rommel advance towards Egypt day by day, almost the next day after it happened. If Egypt falls, the British West Indies will be in the war within a week. Now you will get the news before the *Advocate*. I do not want you to excite the population, and I do not want you to tell them anything about hoarding or anything like that. I want it played down because there is nothing we can do about it. If Egypt falls, we are in the war.'[3]

What happened at that time was this: Italy was never satisfied with

Headline from the Barbados Observer

the division of the spoils after World War I. Mussolini invaded Ethiopia in 1935–36 and the Ethiopians under Selassie defeated the Italians and chased them out, but then the Italians went back in with poison gas and overran the country.

When World War II started in 1939, the first thing the British did was to drive the Italians out of Ethiopia and Eritrea into Somaliland. Part of Libya was also occupied. Then the Germans under Rommel came into North Africa to join the Italians and they started driving the British from the territory which they had taken in Libya.

Up to that time we were not in the actual battle. Fighting was going on along the North African coast with fortunes changing every week, but we were not in that at all. All we ever had down here were two submarine attacks which were made on the harbours of Bridgetown and Castries. Ships were being sunk in the Atlantic, and survivors came ashore here.

The Americans had not yet come into the war, but Roosevelt immediately saw what was involved in terms of America's safety and he arranged with the British to give them fifty old destroyers in return for permission to erect bases in Bermuda, St. Lucia, Antigua, Trinidad and Guiana. (I saw the one in Guiana, Atkinson Field.) My brother, Lisle, was involved in recruiting people to work on the bases. These were intended to defend these islands in case there was ever an invasion by the Germans.

Roosevelt also started sending tremendous war equipment to Africa for the British. Rommel tried to get more soldiers and equipment from Hitler, who never understood the importance of the war in North Africa and refused to give Rommel what he wanted, while America was pumping all kinds of war materials into the area. It was only because the Americans helped the British to stop Rommel from reaching Egypt that we did not become involved in the actual fighting.

It could be said that the logistics were against such an undertaking because German planes did not have the range to come from Dakar to South America. But Bushe was absolutely sure, from the information he got, that this was the plan.

Notes

1   Edward Keith Walcott (1892-1981) was generally regarded as 'the most powerful man in Barbados' when, as Attorney General between 1936 and 1946, he sat on the Executive Committee and was the leader of government business in the House of Assembly. He represented the parish of St. James for over twenty years.

2   Erskine Rueil Latourette (Sir Erskine) Ward (1900 - 1981) later served as

Judge in Guyana, Chief Justice in Belize, and Speaker of the Federal House of Representatives. In 1963 he returned to active politics, joining the DLP and serving as Minister without portfolio in the Cabinet in 1964 to 1965.

3   During the war, a dossier was kept at Government House on the media personnel responsible for publishing the news. Crawford was labelled the main local apostle of class hatred and antagonism to British rule and institutions, was suspected of links with the Communists, and he was therefore a marked man.

CHAPTER 5

Making of the Politician/The 1937 Riots

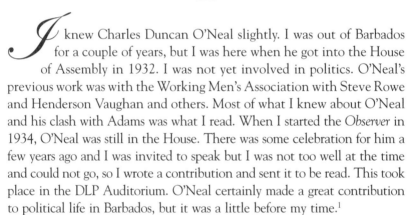

I knew Charles Duncan O'Neal slightly. I was out of Barbados for a couple of years, but I was here when he got into the House of Assembly in 1932. I was not yet involved in politics. O'Neal's previous work was with the Working Men's Association with Steve Rowe and Henderson Vaughan and others. Most of what I knew about O'Neal and his clash with Adams was what I read. When I started the *Observer* in 1934, O'Neal was still in the House. There was some celebration for him a few years ago and I was invited to speak but I was not too well at the time and could not go, so I wrote a contribution and sent it to be read. This took place in the DLP Auditorium. O'Neal certainly made a great contribution to political life in Barbados, but it was a little before my time.[1]

Marcus Garvey also was before my time. I would say that when the Garvey campaign was rampant in Barbados, the original movers would have been John Beckles and people like him.[2] I came into politics long after Garvey started the movement in America and my connection with him was nil; he had no influence on me at all. My only connection with him would have been when he came here in October 1937, and John Beckles and James Martineau and a few other people arranged for him to make a public appearance in Queen's Park. That evening I went to the meeting and, after the meeting, Martineau invited a few of us to his house to entertain Garvey. Martineau lived at the corner of Beckwith and Bay Streets in the same house in which the Barbados Labour Party (BLP) was founded.

It would seem to me that, to a great extent, my involvement in politics was inspired by T. Albert Marryshow of Grenada and his *West Indian* newspaper. I used to meet Marryshow at a house on Saturday nights in St. George's, where the young people went to listen to music and dance and lose themselves. Marryshow had some interest in one of the ladies of the house and he used to be there. He and I used to chat from time to time. Of course, I met him several times after that. I think that, after Grenada, the first time I met him was in Jamaica, in the

Clement Payne

1940s. He and I were at the conference (the Caribbean Labour Congress) financed by West Indians in New York – a group called the West Indies Defence Committee. They raised funds to host a conference of labour and progressive leaders in Kingston, Jamaica, prior to the Montego Bay

Conference on West Indian Federation. Incidentally, I remember that one morning he and I toured a place called Denham Town. We had never seen such poverty in all our lives. Jamaicans were living in boxes, in trees, and in holes dug in the earth lined with cardboard. Living down there was actually horrid. I had never seen anything like it in Barbados.

Marryshow used to come here from time to time, but the last time I saw him I was passing through Grenada on a boat and went to see him at his house in "The Rosery". He was a fairly old man then, and not doing too well, but his newspaper,

Marcus Garvey

Albert Marryshow

The West Indian, really influenced me to a great extent. At that time in Grenada nobody took the morning cup of cocoa without first reading *The West Indian*. Marryshow was apparently running a campaign against the Governor, Sir Hilary Blood, and Sir Frederick Seaton James, the Assistant Colonial Secretary. The headlines on mornings in *The West Indian* used to be 'BLOOD AND SEATON JAMES MUST GO, WE DON'T WANT THEM HERE AT ALL'. Marryshow and his *West Indian* were irreconcilably anti-colonial, and throughout its forty-one years of existence my newspaper, the *Barbados Observer*, stringently reflected this policy.

Blood was later appointed Governor of Barbados. Marryshow's newspaper in Grenada was certainly a force to be reckoned with and the man himself was quite a figure in the politics of the era. He was the Grenada delegate to the first West Indian Conference on Federation held in Dominica in 1932. Trinidad was represented by one of its national heroes, Captain Cipriani. I remember attending his funeral in Trinidad when he died. Barbados was represented by Charlie Elder and J.S. Sainsbury. Marryshow made several visits to New York and to England demanding West Indian political independence, the end to colonialism, and a better deal for the West Indian colonies.

With the publication of the *Observer*, I became more deeply involved with politics, and particularly after the 1937 riots took place. As a matter of fact, I had written an editorial the very Saturday before the riots took place in which I had warned the Government seriously that, unless very constructive improvement took place in the social and economic conditions of the society immediately, there was bound to be a revolt of some sort. There had been, before that, outbreaks in St. Vincent, St. Kitts and Trinidad, and Jamaica came afterwards. I was in New York in 1938 when the Jamaica riots took place.

The weekly *Observer*, on the Saturday before the riots took place in 1937, carried the banner headline 'BLACK DOGS ONLY BARK, THEY

Newspaper Headline

CANNOT BITE'. This really was a quotation from the remarks of Lieutenant-Colonel Hickling, an American, who was in charge of Apex Oilfields Ltd. in Trinidad. When the riots broke out in Trinidad's oil fields, it was a serious revolt because there was a police chap, Corporal King, who was much hated and despised by the workers and they actually poured a tin of kerosene oil on him and lit him, burning him to death. When it was reported to the Lieutenant-Colonel that there was trouble among the oil workers, his reply was: 'Well, don't take them on. Black dogs don't bite, they only bark.'

The riots were an important factor in my movement to politics. I got so deeply involved with the riots and the aftermath, the court cases and associated activities, that I had no time for myself. I remember I had got very active in tennis at that time. We would go on afternoons to play, but my evenings and nights became so occupied with political matters and meetings that I had no time even for that. A long time afterwards, when one of my brothers, Cecil, got a teaching appointment in Tobago, I told him to take my racquets because I had no time for them. The riots were in 1937, and in 1938 the attempt was made to organize the people in Barbados when the Progressive League was started. In 1939 I was actually asked to run for a seat in the House of Assembly.

I can never forget the events which took place on the day of the riots. It was a Monday morning. A telephone call that morning from a proofreader for the *Barbados Observer* informed me about the disturbances in the city. So I ran to the car and hastened down to town.

The first peculiar thing I observed when I got to what was then called the "Old Bridge", the Duncan O'Neal Bridge, was the late Sir Clyde Archer, a City Magistrate, and a small posse (a small bodyguard of armed men) going over the bridge. He seemed to me to be trembling in his boots and had a sheet of paper in his hands. I was informed that he was going to read the Riot Act somewhere near the market in Fairchild Street. A similar procedure was being enacted in another part of the City by Magistrate Frank Field. I do not know where exactly. Some years ago, a representative of the *Nation* newspaper approached me in connection with the disturbances and I told them to see Clyde Archer because he would probably have been able to tell them more. Sir Clyde told the *Nation* that, on that morning in question, he was given this bodyguard (some of the men were fire brigade men, I think) who had never handled a rifle in all their lives. Going over the bridge, somewhere along the route, one of the fire brigade men stumbled and a shot was fired off. So Clyde did not know if he had to be more afraid of the bodyguards or the rioters. In any case, the protesters were not armed.

I got into town and was informed that all the stores were being closed tight and everybody was running out of the city. The Riot Act had been read. Business houses were ordered to close and all the workers were to go home. When I got to my office, some of the staff told me they were sure they had seen a machine gun mounted on top of the building adjacent to mine, which then housed the Telephone Company on Lucas Street, and they thought that we should close up the place and go home. I told them, 'Sure, you go ahead. I will stay around here for a while.' I stayed and I had half of the big doors opened and, later in the day, it must have been early afternoon, my proof reader, a young chap in his early twenties called Dorian Herbert, who recently died in England, and a journalist called Archie Greaves, walked into my office. Archie Greaves was quite a character. He worked more or less with the *Herald* newspaper. He used to contribute a column entitled 'Lizzie and Joe' every week in the new weekly *Herald*, and he also contributed a report on various Anglican church services about the country.

To get back to the morning of the riots: Greaves and Herbert came to my place in the early afternoon and we were talking and I said, 'I heard a report a little while ago that there is a chap lying in Suttle Street with his

Riot Scene from Lower Broad Street

insides blasted open by a shotgun or something. I think we should go and have a look at him if we can get down there.' So Greaves, Herbert and I left Lucas Street and went down to Suttle Street. True enough, there was this chap lying on the ground with a terrific hole in his side with the blood oozing out and a million flies around him. I do not know how long he had been there. Nobody seemed to know who he was. We passed him and left him there. When we got around to the end of Suttle Street, we heard a terrific lot of shouting from a house around the corner before the turn to Broad Street. A young man, who came from St. Thomas, had come into town that day on some errand, for what reason nobody knows. He was shot by the police and he crawled upstairs to the verandah of a house behind where Plantations Ltd is now, and he died there. His mother heard the news and she came down. She had heard where the body was and she went upstairs and, as soon as she saw him, she started a loud wailing and shouting and carrying on. The noise began to attract people from the street behind St. Mary's Church and they started to gather. They saw Herbert and Greaves and me out there too, and in a short while there was a little crowd. Crowds were banned by the reading of the Riot Act. Therefore, as soon as this little crowd began to gather, I said, 'Herbert, we got to get out of here. There will be trouble around here just now.' At the time there was a police station in Cheapside near the public market.

Apparently, somebody told the police down there that a crowd was gathering behind St. Mary's Church, so a few of the police started coming up the road, shooting as they came. Greaves at that time must have been in his middle fifties, Herbert was in his early twenties and I, too, was in my twenties. I said, 'Herbert we can't afford to let anything happen to Greaves. You hold one hand of Greaves and I will hold the other hand and we will race up Broad Street, duck through Harrison's Alley and get back to the *Barbados Observer.*' So he held one hand and I held the other and we started running up Broad Street. By this time, the police up by the Public Buildings had heard the shots coming from St. Mary's and had started down Broad Street shooting. As soon as a few shots went over our heads, you know, although we were half Greaves's age, Greaves gave a tug and we could not catch him at all! When Herbert and I got to the entrance of Harrison's Alley, Greaves was already at the corner of Swan Street, and by the time we got to the *Barbados Observer,* he was there already. I had the key and we unlocked the door and went in.

After a while, the two of them left and I was thinking about going home when Dan Blackett walked into my office. Then, a short while afterwards, a chap called Hinkitch Bell, Gordon Bell's brother, came in. A little later Grantley Adams walked in. We were at the main door talking. All of a sudden we saw a woman with a tray of fruits on her head coming up Swan Street at the corner where Barbados Hardware is now. A policeman came down Swan Street and, for no reason whatsoever, fired three shots at her. She dropped down dead at the corner and the tray with the fruits splattered all over the street. Subsequently, I understood that she came from Brittons Hill. She was a Seventh Day Adventist. I actually heard her name because a member of the church, Brenda Prescod, who is still alive, told me that she knew this woman well. I knew the policeman who shot the woman. He turned and he saw Blackett, Adams, Bell and myself at the door of the *Barbados Observer* building and shouted, 'Mr. Crawford, you know damn well that no door should be open and everything should be shut.' He fired some shots at the *Barbados Observer* building and they lodged in the wall. Grantley, Blackett and myself ran and hid behind the printing press.

The Riot Act warned people against congregating or assembling in crowds. So the policeman had no reason at all for shooting the woman. She was a middle-aged woman. I saw her face as she lay dead in the street. She used to go and buy fruits. What she did was not troubling anybody at all. He was just crazy. Of course, he got no punishment because she was just unfortunately caught in the city that morning.

Before the disturbances were over, there were fourteen persons shot dead in Barbados. Others were arrested for digging potatoes.

Newspaper Headline

Unfortunately, in those days there was no legal aid available. When Clement Payne was first arrested, I went to Grantley Adams to see what could be done. According to what Grantley told the Disturbances Commission, Payne had no money. It was only after Cephas Mahon and Nicey Belgrave passed around Mahon's hat and raised the $52.00 to pay Adams that he agreed to appear for Payne. He got him off. Despite this, Payne was spirited on to a ship and sent back to Trinidad.[3] After that, there was nobody to represent those charged and they could not get anyone to defend them because Grantley had gone away (to Britain).

One lawyer, Henderson Clarke, took some cases but he charged so much money that the families of the accused had to sell their donkeys and their carts and little chattel houses to raise money. He told his clients to go in court and plead guilty. I was so mad with him that I do not think I ever spoke to him afterwards. When he died, I never even published a word about it in the *Barbados Observer*, nor did I write an obituary because of the way he just squeezed people during the riot.

Some of those who used to hold the meetings along with Payne were considered ringleaders. Those who spoke in the meetings prior to the disturbances were charged with sedition. There was Israel Lovell, a carpenter, who used to be in the Working Men's Association with Dr O'Neal. Hilton Vaughan defended him. Lovell was told to plead guilty and, to his surprise, he got five years. There was a chap called "Brain" Alleyne who was a local preacher, but he was no seditionist. Another alleged ringleader, Menzies

Chase, got a light sentence. There was another man, Sebro, who was a boatman on the wharf. He was very active with Duncan O'Neal, but he got off. Then, of course, there was Ulric Grant who got the maximum sentence of ten years with special confinement. "Brain" Alleyne and Israel Lovell got five years.[4]

I regarded Grant's sentence as very harsh because he just used to stop at a few of the meetings held by Payne. But it was said, I do not know if it is correct, that he had been deported from America because he had been in conflict with the authorities there and I think, because of that, the local authorities were more severe in dealing with him than with anybody else.[5]

Immediately after Grant's trial, I applied to the court and got a copy of the trial proceedings and sent them off to Creech Jones who was then the shadow minister for the colonies in the British Parliament. The Labour Party was in opposition, and I asked Creech Jones to raise the question of Grant's sentence in Parliament, which he did, and he said it was savage, outrageous, and unjust. He raised the devil in the Commons about it and the same evening – it was a Friday – it came over the BBC, and I heard it. Within half an hour, the Island's Registrar came to me with a message from the Chief Justice, Allan Collymore, asking me not to publish it. I said to the Registrar, 'Look here, man, Collymore had no right giving Grant ten years. This will appear on the front page of the *Barbados Observer* tomorrow.' That Saturday morning, I had a headline across the front page

'CREECH JONES CALLED GRANT'S SENTENCE SAVAGE AND OUTRAGEOUS'.

Collymore did not speak to me for years. The first time was when we were in attendance at the King's Birthday Parade at the Garrison, and officials were being entertained in the Officers' Mess upstairs of the Drill Hall. A chap from St Philip, who had emigrated to America and had become quite a big officer in the American army then fighting in Korea, had been flown down here to see his sick father before he died. I took him with me to the Drill Hall that day. Collymore, seeing his uniform and his medals, came up and said: 'Mr. Crawford, let me meet your friend. Who is your friend? I was in the British Army during World War 1, you know.' He took the officer and introduced him to some people. This censure on Collymore in the House of Commons actually delayed his receipt of the knighthood he should have had as the Chief Justice.

I had also raised the question of Grant on the floor of the Assembly several times saying that he should be released. Eventually he was released long before the ten years expired. But the trial and sentencing of Grant, among others, received a lot of attention outside the West Indies.[6] I remember that it interested a British journalist, Nancy Cunard, a relative of Sir Edward Cunard from Glitter Bay, St James. They were connected with the Cunard Steamship Lines. She was in Spain reporting the Spanish Civil War between Franco and the Republicans for the *Manchester Guardian* and, fresh from that assignment, she came down to Barbados to spend some time with her relatives. She phoned me one day and said she wanted to see me. We made an appointment to meet at my office. So she came up and the first thing she said was: 'Well, I want to see Grant. I want to talk to Grant.' So I took her to Glendairy Prison to see him.

Grant lived for a couple of years after he came out from prison but I think he was not in the best of health before that and the hardships of the confinement to penal servitude probably hastened his death. 'Brain' Alleyne had a wife and quite a few children. She came to me every Saturday at the newspaper and said she had nothing at all, and that the children were starving. So I organized a small group to give her money every Saturday so that she could buy food for herself and her children, and carry food to Glendairy Prison for her husband and Grant. I got 'Chrissie' Brathwaite, Martineau, Dentist Storey and a few more together, and I used to send her every Saturday to them and they would give her a few dollars. There were also a few stores in Swan Street which used to give clothing for them. I remember very well three stores, all of them owned or run by Grenadians. N.E. Wilson used to give her some things. At the corner of Swan Street, where Barbados Hardware is now, was a store run by a man called St. Bernard. At the other corner of Swan Street and Bolton Lane was a store called David Slinger and Company, and the man who ran it was a Grenadian called Sebright who used to give her pajamas and shirts. This went on for some time. But in 1938, I was invited to New York by the West Indies Defence Committee to talk about conditions in the West Indies, so Barry Springer, the barber, offered to take over the responsibility for the collection for Alleyne's wife on Saturdays. However, before I came back from New York, it was stopped because Barry said people gave a lot of trouble to contribute money after I went away and he could not get enough, so he could not bother with it anymore and stopped it.

The situation (as far as the disturbances were concerned) was different in the country districts. Most of the cases were for breaking shops and entering and stealing food and digging potatoes and yams and foodstuff from the plantations. There was no armed resistance, although the Volunteer Force was called out. An officer of the Volunteer Force was put in charge of the Cable office at Dover, and members of that force then came down and guarded the Electric Company in the Garrison; and the officer told the men to shoot on sight and then ask questions afterwards. He did very well in the government service later on. There was no armed revolution. You would not have found one gun among all the people themselves.

The Riot Act was read in the early morning and it was early afternoon when I saw the woman shot at the corner , where Barbados Hardware is now. When the policeman fired five shots at the *Barbados Observer* building, it must have been around 2:00 p.m. But I do not know when the man I saw on Suttle Street was shot, or the boy. But I imagine that people must have been shot even on the second day too. The people with guns (the police and volunteers) were trigger-happy. In the absence of modern day communication, many people would not have heard or known about the Riot Act, and they went about their business as usual.

I could not say positively why so many were shot because I do not know most of the cases that happened, but the woman I saw was just a harmless citizen, and the boy in the upstairs building on St Mary's Street, or around there, was a boy who had come down on an errand for his mother. He was no rioter. The man in Suttle Street was probably a harmless man as well. Most of the cases that went to court were for pillaging and shop breaking. No one was charged for having firearms, not even those who were arrested for sedition. There was no question of armed resistance from the people. There were Special Juries who, it would seem, if you were quoting the Bible, would have said that you were disturbing the population. I think that Lovell had a lawyer, but my recollection was that, although he had a lawyer, he was told to plead guilty. Lovell was a harmless carpenter and he was a disciple in the Dr O'Neal movement. I want to be accurate, but my recollection is that Lovell pleaded guilty and was still given a long sentence in jail (five years). He had done nothing at all to warrant this punishment. I think he went crazy and died in the mental hospital.

On the morning after Payne had been deported, the disturbance in Bridgetown was sparked off by a report that his child had been killed by the police. People went down Broad Street smashing show windows and turning over cars in the road. Where the fire station is now on Probyn Street, there was a garage called Cole's Garage. They took cars from there and pushed them into the careenage. I actually went to the garage some time afterwards and saw a very good-looking car. I was told it belonged to Dr. Bancroft from Barbarees Hill. There was a good price on it, so I bought the car. I did not know it had been thrown into the sea. It had been excellently repainted. In less than a year it started rusting all over again because of the sea water. So I lost my money.

There is a belief that once the disturbance started in town, some people might have sent messages or moved from town into rural districts saying that something was happening in town and that the rurals should do their own thing. I do not think that any such report was given to the Commission. What people needed was food and money. After the shops were closed, they started digging potatoes and yams and breaking shops. Mr. James Tudor had some shops all over Barbados but he did not prosecute the people who stole his goods.

The sugar planters would not have put arms into the hands of working people in order to protect their plantations. Overseers used to handle rifles from time to time to shoot wild rabbits and hares, but they did not shoot anyone. The fact is that people were opposed to authority and to those who were keeping them in servitude, and their reaction would be to loot and destroy crops. But to say that they had actually been advised from a central force in Bridgetown, or runners were sent to tell them, is not correct. I imagine that most rebellions against authority just spread because people think they can take the law into their own hands. News would not have lacked carriers as buses were running up and down. I do not know whether the Riot Act was read at the police stations in the country as well. I never heard and I never inquired.

If you read the Deane Commission Report, you would not believe that people could live under such terrible conditions. It was a very good report. A planter was asked by the Chairman, Sir George Deane, if the workers on the estates ever got milk in their tea in the morning and he replied, 'Not during the week, but maybe sometimes on Sunday we would send a little milk for them – and, if they are sick they might get a little milk, now and then.'

He was talking about 1937 when the riots took place; and Dr. Hawkins literally told the Commission that the high infant mortality rate was the substitute for family planning. In the newspaper reports, most of the charges against people were for looting shops and digging provisions out of the plantations. But there is no record of any planter or any merchant having been personally attacked or any attempt to destroy government property or anything like that. The people vented their wrath in the city because of the trouble concerning Payne and the reported death of Payne's child (which I am not sure was accurate) and the fact that he had been smuggled aboard the ship by the police and had been deported. They were angry also because of the manner in which his trial was conducted and the sentences imposed.

Payne, Alleyne and Sebro were holding meetings about the place and they used to hold meetings in the Lower Green quite often. I knew them all well because they used lanterns mounted on a stick. At night when they had finished, and I was down at the newspaper office, they would walk in and say, 'Chief, we are going to leave these here until tomorrow night.' So they would put their things in a corner of the place and leave them there. As a matter of fact, there was some confusion between them from time to time. All of them were hard up, and they used to collect a few cents here and there from the crowds. Sometimes a chap had the money and he did not want to share and they could not find him. Some of their speeches were supposed to have been inflammatory. I never went to any of the meetings myself, but they must have had enough effect on the people to arouse indignation to the point where, the morning after Payne's departure, the mob came down rioting.[7]

The two Commissions which reported after the disturbance of 1937 were to have a profound effect on the history of Barbados. The Deane Commission made certain far-reaching recommendations. Its report was named after Sir George Deane but it was supposed to have been largely the work of Erskine Ward.

The Moyne Commission had a great impact on politics in Barbados and it was of tremendous help to the progressive forces. There is no question that this Commission did a very good job and that the investigation was thorough. The report of that Commission was not published until after the war, in 1945, because the British government considered that its revelations were so astounding and incriminating that they dared not publish lest they gave more grist to the Nazi propaganda mill about how they treated the colonies.

Commissions have special uses. If you want to delay action on a matter, or if you want to find the facts, or if you want to put up a smoke screen behind which you can hide delayed action, a commission is appointed. In the case of the Moyne Commission, there were one or two good men on it. Lord Moyne, himself, was not reactionary. But I would say that if the recommendations of the Moyne Commission in total, or even to a greater extent, had been implemented, conditions would have been very much improved much sooner than they were. As I said earlier, the conclusive recommendations of the Deane Commission were supposed to have been the work of Erskine Ward who was a liberal, although the Commission was named after Sir George Deane who was a planter. Erskine Ward was a member of the House between 1930–1932. He got there on a Progressive ticket. But the story is that the planters got to his father and asked him whether he intended to permit that son of his to ruin the country. His father then persuaded him to take a magistracy. So he went out of politics and eventually became a judge in Guyana and Chief Justice in British Honduras.

I myself repeatedly took things from the Commissions' recommendations and tried to get the government to implement them in the House. For instance, the Moyne Commission was very annoyed over the fact that hardly anything was done to improve the social conditions of workers in the sugar cane industry, which was the main industry in the island. They recommended that a levy of two shillings a ton be placed on sugar and the money devoted to providing welfare schemes, playing fields and social amenities for the agricultural districts, after the pattern set by the Coal Board in England where there was a small levy on every ton of coal produced. That money was devoted exclusively to providing social welfare schemes and amenities for coal miners. I tried repeatedly on the floor of the Assembly by resolution and otherwise to get the government to levy that two shillings a ton for every ton of sugar produced to provide playing fields for the agricultural areas. They never did it. Eventually the British government itself, in increasing the sugar price one year, allocated certain proportions for specific purposes. Three different levies were included in the sugar price and deducted before it was disbursed. One was for welfare for the agricultural labourers, one was for helping the sugar factories to get new machinery, bought from England of course, and the third was for a fund to be placed there in case there was a slump in the price of sugar at any time. It was called the Price Stabilization Fund. These measures were carried out by the British government itself.

At one time there were two banks established for assisting the sugar industry – The Sugar Industry Agricultural Bank and the Peasants' Loan Bank. The Agricultural Bank was established in 1902 after a grant by Joseph Chamberlain of £80,000 to the West Indies. Chamberlain was Secretary of State for the Colonies. He was the father of Neville Chamberlain who was later a British Prime Minister. The Barbados planters did not distribute the money among themselves but established a bank instead. The bank loaned money to the individual planters and factories every year to cover running expenses. They repaid it when the crops were reaped. But there was no assistance for the small peasants and farmers and, when I was canvassing in St Philip, most of the peasant farmers told me that they were afraid to vote for me. They could not borrow money any more from the sugar factories or the sugar planters to assist them in carrying on during the year until they reaped the canes. One of my first promises was to see that the government establish a Peasants' Loan Bank, specifically for the purpose of assisting small farmers with loans for buying livestock, manure and paying workers, etc. until they got the canes reaped, so that they could be independent of the big sugar factory people.[8]

Notes

1   Dr Charles Duncan O'Neal (1876-1936), National Hero of Barbados, was in many respects the founder of the labour movement and of mass politics in Barbados. His political activity through the Democratic League (1924), the Workingman's Association (1926), and in the House of Assembly (1932-1936) prepared the way for the political and social changes of the 1940s and 1950s.

2   John Beresford Beckles (1874–1954) was a prominent black entrepreneur, humanitarian, social and political activist. He was the leading Garveyite in Barbados, a political associate of O'Neal, and a successful politician at the parochial (vestry) level.

3   Clement Osbourne Payne (1904–1941), National Hero of Barbados, was mainly responsible for the political ferment which erupted in the riots and disturbances in Barbados in July 1937. His attempts to mobilize the urban workers resulted in his illegal deportation to Trinidad. This perceived persecution triggered the labour revolt.

4   Menzies Chase received a sentence of nine months' imprisonment for sedition, in sharp contrast to the sentences of five and ten years' imprisonment imposed on Mortimer Skeete, Grant, Alleyne and Lovell for similar offences.

5   Ulric Grant had been deported from US in March 1934 after being thrice convicted on attempted burglary and petty larceny charges.

6   The campaign for the remission of the sentences imposed on the 'political prisoners' continued well into 1940. It was carried in UK by the Labour Party, by the National Council for Civil Liberties, and by the League of Coloured Peoples. Locally, Crawford and the other Progressives, notably Grantley Adams, James A. Tudor, H.A. Vaughan, J.T.C. Ramsay, J.A. Martineau and 'Chrissie' Brathwaite, kept up the pressure through individual and group petitions to the Colonial Office and questions in the House of

Assembly. The continued pressure yielded mixed results. In August 1939, Lovell was released after serving less than one year of his five-year sentence because of his previous good character, his advancing age (60), and evident reformation. Neither Grant nor Alleyne benefitted immediately from this humanitarian impulse. Grant was still perceived as 'a bad lot'; and Alleyne's prison record was described as 'not exemplary'.

7   Clearly Crawford, like Adams, H.A. Vaughan and other 'progressive' politicians, did not comprehend, until after the fact, the impact that Payne was making on a situation which had 'combustible' elements. All of them seemed convinced that Payne was a mere opportunist.

8   The Peasants' Loan Bank (later called the Agricultural Credit Bank) was established in 1937 but it was not until the early 1950s that its loans made much impact on the peasant agricultural sector.

CHAPTER 6

Early Relationship With Grantley Adams

$\mathcal{E}$rnest Mottley sued me for libel in September 1937[1]. The background on that is that, during the riots, Grantley Adams claimed that a car had passed up the hill by his house one night and that a man had fired shots at his home. I think that he also claimed that his gardener or night watchman was wounded. The case went to court, and I do not think anything came out of it. Adams told me that the man had said during the trial that Mottley was driving the car. In the *Advocate* nothing like that was printed. But Adams came to my office and said that the *Advocate* had misrepresented the facts of the case and that he wanted the entire thing published. He said that he would supply me with that part of the evidence which, added to the *Advocate*'s small report, would give a more accurate account of what had taken place, and that he would send me this additional information in the afternoon. Later that day, his messenger, Clement, brought me this additional information in Adams's handwriting, and I published it along with the other details of the case. Mottley promptly sued me for criminal libel because, he said, those words had never been used in the court, and the Magistrate, C.B. Archer, also confirmed that those words had never been used in his court. So Mottley brought a criminal charge against me, and it was set down for the Assizes.

There were not very many lawyers in the country in those days, and there was nobody I could get to take the case here, so I had to bring a lawyer from Trinidad, a man called Louis Wharton. He came up for the initial case but then, before the Assizes, he wanted the full fee and I did not have the money, so Mrs. Grantley Adams and myself and Edwy Talma went down to 'Lemon Grove' and borrowed the initial deposit from James A. Tudor. Mrs Adams assured me that she would see to it that her husband paid it back.[2] I had to get friends to back the note at the Royal Bank to get the remainder of money. In the meantime, Adams had gone away and he did not come back until after the trial.

E.D. Mottley

Grantley and I had been in constant contact daily (at one time we would ring each other almost every night to discuss what was going on with the riots), yet he had never mentioned his going away to me. As a matter of fact, one Saturday morning, he was in my office talking and two clerks from the court, Dixie Daniel and Rawle Sharpe, walked in to say hello to me. Dixie said to Adams, 'Grantley, did you get your ticket? When are you going?' Grantley replied, 'On Monday.' So I turned to Grantley and said, 'Are you going away?' He said, 'Yes.' I said, 'Where did you get the money from?' He said, 'Well, I got James Tudor to back a note at the Royal Bank for me.' So I said, 'With all these people in jail you are leaving the island? Man, I wouldn't come and see you off.' The morning that he left, the persons who saw him off were his wife and a man called Dan Blackett.

Two neighbours of his, a brother and sister who lived in Spooners Hill, were spending time at some mutual friends on Bay Street, called the Estwicks. They told me that, just before Adams went away, he had told them that he had heard that the Crown Prosecutors were trying to lodge actions against himself and me in connection with the riots and he was clearing out, but he was not going to tell me anything because I would want to go too. But it occurred to me, subsequently, that the Mottley trial had a lot to do with his going also, because I had his manuscript in his own handwriting and, if he had been charged, he would have had to be found guilty and, as a lawyer, he could have been struck off the roll. The Crown officials knew that I was not the author of the allegation because it had come out during the trial in the lower court that Adams had written the manuscript containing the allegation against Mottley and had sent it by his messenger to me. It was said that, if I surrendered the manuscript, the proceedings would be minimized. So I had to give the manuscript to the Solicitor-General, 'Jubie' Reece, and the proceedings were minimized after that.[3]

When Grantley left for London, the Colonial Office had already announced the appointment of the Royal (Moyne) Commission. I have heard it said that he indicated that he knew a few Labour and/or Liberal Members of Parliament with whom he wanted to discuss matters. But when he left here, he had no idea at all of going to the Colonial Office.

After he left for England, I called Brathwaite and Martineau and others from the 'progressives' together and told them, 'I think we are going to have to make it appear that we have sent him to the Colonial office.' I suggested that we prepare a petition and get signatures to it and carry it to the Governor. I published that petition on the editorial page of the *Barbados Observer* the Saturday after he left.[4] I remember very well. Down through the years, several times I thought I should have exposed this, but it would have appeared that I also personally had misled the people, because the idea was mine really and the others agreed. Talma drafted the petition in part, and we had people going around getting signatures to it. Then we took this petition with all these signatures to the Governor, Sir Mark Young, requesting him to make the necessary representation immediately to London to ensure that Adams had an interview with the Colonial Secretary. Young refused to do it. He said, 'I am doing no such thing. You all are aware that the British government has already announced that they are appointing a Royal Commission to come down here to investigate conditions. So what is the point of Adams telling them what they are coming to see for themselves?' We went back downstairs – 'Chrissie' Brathwaite, Martineau, Cummins, myself, and, I think, Dan Blackett. We were in the yard talking and I said to Chrissie, 'Man, Chrissie, we can't allow Young to come and dictate to us, telling us what we can do. He is only the Governor. He doesn't represent the people. Let's go back upstairs and tell him that if Adams comes back without seeing the Colonial Secretary, we are going to send him back again.' Chrissie said, 'Well, if you feel so, go back and tell him nuh!,' I went back upstairs alone and told Young that, if he did not send on this petition to the Colonial Office, we would send Adams back again. He said, 'Well, Mr. Crawford, if that is the attitude you are going to adopt, I will do it.' He sent the petition to England and that made Adams a hell of a hero.[5]

I have not read any of F.A. Hoyos's books myself, but I understand that he tries to make it appear that Adams left the island to go to England to represent the people. What gets me very annoyed is the way that Hoyos distorts these things. He rang me one day and said he was collecting some information for another volume that he was writing and he wanted to give me and the *Observer* full credit because he had drawn heavily on it for information and this time he was going to see that I got full credit for it. I told him that he was distorting history and other people were now involved in writing the facts and would expose him for what he was. He asked who was doing it as he wanted to compare notes with them and 'to correct any mistakes he had made. Then his exact words to me were, 'You mean at long last somebody is debunking the old man?'[6]

Adams went to England because he thought he could be prosecuted. Although there was no actual case against him, Darnley 'Brain' Alleyne, who was arrested during the riots and charged for sedition, told me, and he must have told other people too, that the night before the riots started, when Payne was shipped away and Payne's child was reported to have been killed by the police in Jessamy Lane, the people sent and called Adams to come down because an angry mob was collecting there. Adams told Alleyne, 'You go and start a meeting in the Lower Green, and as soon as I get through here, I will come down there and join you all.' Alleyne was arrested. He also told me that Adams came and saw him the next morning and said, 'Brain, don't worry, I will soon get you out.' The next thing he heard, Adams was in England.

That meeting was supposed to have sparked off the riot the next morning, because Menzies Chase (I think he used to work with 'Jubie' Reece as a messenger) was supposed to have said at the meeting, 'Tonight is a funny day. . . .' I suppose that Adams's statement could be stretched to mean that he told Darnley Alleyne to go and start something.

Adams was supposed to come back at the end of the month of October, but he said he was ill and had pneumonia and did not come back until after the sessions were over in November. We made a big thing of it when he came back. We were trying to give the impression to the authorities – the white planters and merchants – that we had somebody we could support to take up our cause. We had built him up as this hero abroad and we had conveyed the impression, quite unjustifiably, that we had sent him up to England. There were thousands of people on the wharf when he arrived.

Martineau and Cummins and all of them then suggested that it would be a good idea to make a public collection to give him a car because he had a little two-seater, and they figured they would give him a bigger car and make the Conservatives feel that we were really doing something. It took some time to collect the money and, when Martineau and Cummins took the car, a second-hand Hillman from McEnearney, they could not pay all the money because the collection had not yet reached the target. The car was presented in Queen's Park before a huge and appreciative crowd.

When people saw Adams driving about in it, they refused to subscribe anymore. The Executive of the Progressive League decided to hold a dance in Queen's Park to raise the balance of the money. They proposed to give me part of the money raised from the dance to pay the loan which was owed to the bank for my libel case. I worked very hard in promoting the dance, but they barely raised enough to finish paying for the car. Martineau and Cummins were responsible for it, and naturally they did not want to owe anything afterwards. I never got a cent. They left me holding the bag. I went to Adams about the money since his wife had sworn that she would try to see that he paid the money to the bank. He refused to pay a cent of the costs involved in the case. I do not think he paid back Tudor the money he had borrowed to go to England. That was the story I heard. I got so annoyed that I disassociated myself from the Progressive League after that.

I think that Adams learned the lesson from Payne – what it meant to have the masses behind you – because before that he had tried to get a government job as Solicitor-General. I think he applied when Frank Holder got it but I know for a fact that he applied when Reece got it. I never used it against him because I had supported him for the job editorially in the *Barbados Observer*. This was before the riots – probably in early 1937. It was after the riots that he began to appreciate the value of the support of the working class.

He really had no connection with the people who were involved in the riots. At first he refused to appear in court for Payne because, of course, Payne could not pay him. It was only after Cephas Mahon, ('Talk yuh talk'), and Nicey Belgrave passed around Mahon's hat and raised the $52.00 to pay Adams that he agreed to appear for Payne. Despite this, he was looming on the horizon as the sort of person who could take charge of the reform movement at that time because, when he left the island, the Progressives were at a loss as to what to do, and that is why we thought of sending the petition. When he returned, therefore, we were not thinking of making him our leader because there was no party or anything then. We were not thinking at all about supplanting 'Chrissie' Brathwaite who had long been accepted as one of the leading 'progressives' and was supposed to become the leader of the Party that was started afterwards.[7] We were thinking of getting a good strong man in the struggle. Adams, however, assumed the leadership by destroying Brathwaite and getting rid of the other party leaders.

I remember the libel action against Clennell Wickham that was brought in 1930 by a Walter Bayley, a merchant and jeweller in town, who was the father of the well-known Dr Bayley who had the clinic at 23 Beckles Road. In those days Adams was the editor of the *Agricultural Reporter*. I was quite

"Chrissie" Brathwaite

a young fellow and I recall that Wickham wrote in one of his columns that, 'In his present state of political health, Grantley Adams was a menace to any community'. Wickham took very strong sides in the election in St. Philip when Adams clashed with Hilton Vaughan and the clash resulted of course in the re-election of the two conservatives for St Philip, Dr Hawkins and Mr Skeete, who were both Directors of the *Agricultural Reporter* which Adams edited. So the feud between Wickham and Adams was well known and when Wickham, it was alleged, wrote an article which Bayley regarded as libellous, Bayley took him to court and retained the services of Adams. Adams took the case, some thought with great relish, because it gave him the opportunity to get at Wickham. The manner in which he began to cross-examine Wickham during the Bayley trial is significant: ' . . . . So you are Clennell Warwick Wickham, Warwick, the king maker?' The result of the case was a foregone conclusion because he had a Special Jury, more or less all white. In those days, if a Special Jury was desired, either side could apply for it and get it. With an all-white jury, Wickham had no chance at all. The *Herald* was destroyed.

After that, Wickham was in Barbados for quite a while and at one time he tried to publish a monthly magazine, the *Outlook*. I do not think it lasted long. He wrote for a weekly publication the *Advocate* put out. He then went down to Grenada to work with Marryshow's newspaper, *The West Indian*, and in a short time he died in Grenada (in September 1938).[8]

Clennell Wickham

His admirers organized the Clennell Wickham Association and decided in 1943 to hold a memorial service for him at the home of James A. Tudor at 'Lemon Grove', St Michael. I went down to the service and, to my surprise, Adams went down there and eulogized Wickham, even after he might have been the instrument that was used, more or less, to destroy him and the old *Herald*. Under the caption 'A Grave Error,' I wrote an editorial for the *Barbados Observer* (on October 23, 1943), and I remember saying that Wickham must have been turning in his grave on hearing all these eulogies from Grantley Adams. I said that Wickham could never have forgiven Adams for the part he played, in virtually chasing him out of the island.

Adams prosecuted me for libel. He engaged the services of a Special Jury and got H.O.B. Wooding from Trinidad to represent him. I got the services of a man called 'Jubie' Reece. In any case, the result was a foregone conclusion, and the jury awarded Adams £1,500 and costs, which was a lot of money in those days. He registered the judgement and allowed it to remain nearly ten years. I think he then got Deighton Ward, who was a practising barrister at the time, and Rex Gill to call on me for the amount with interest. He did that from sheer viciousness.

Sir Grantley Adams

Nobody understood how I could forgive Adams and join a

coalition with him in 1946. I did not have the money of course, so I had to go to Ernest Mottley who told me he would borrow the money for me from Carrington and Sealy, a firm of solicitors in town but I would have to pay him interest. In those days, £1,500 was a lot of money although it sounds like nothing now. In those days, a civil servant joined the service at a salary of $20.00 per month and a lot of headmasters were getting $40.00 and $50.00 per month.

It took me a long time to repay such a big debt. I think that, when it was due, I went to old man Boyce at Yearwood and Boyce. He was the senior partner for years. He was a great man. When I heard he was dying, I had to shed a tear.

Adams wanted to get me bankrupt, to begin with, because he put me in court. Everybody said I would be bankrupt because they knew I could not pay the money. And, if you were declared a bankrupt, you could not then sit in the House of Assembly according to law. That is what happened with Wickham in his libel case. Wickham was declared bankrupt when the *Herald* closed down. But with the popularity of the *Barbados Observer* at the time, I do not think Adams could have risked that, so he just let the judgement stay there and collected the money later on. I remember it was Keith Walcott, Attorney-General and leader of the conservative party in the House of Assembly, who said, 'Imagine he's the man who refused a coalition with us and went with Grantley Adams!'

Notes

1   Ernest Deighton Mottley (1907–1973) was a real estate broker and a successful politician particularly at the parish level. He was the first Mayor of Bridgetown (1959), represented Bridgetown in the House of Assembly from 1946 to 1966, and was the leader of the conservative party, the Barbados National Party, in the 1961 elections.

2   James A. Tudor (father of Sir James Tudor) was a successful retail provision merchant who supported progressive causes throughout his life. He provided financial backing and a meeting place (at his home, 'Lemon Grove') for the Progressive League, the Barbados Labour Party and, later, for the fledgling Democratic Labour Party. He also served one term in the House of Assembly during the 1930s.

3   Crawford pleaded guilty to the charge of criminal libel at the Court of Grand Sessions on 12 November 1937. The prosecution, led by E.K. Walcott, the Attorney General, did not oppose a plea for mercy, and the Chief Justice bound over Crawford in his own recognizance for one year.

4   This petition, signed by over two thousand persons, mainly artisans residing all across the island, declared that the petitioners were taxpayers and voters. It emphasized that Adams, 'our most trusted and well-beloved representative', had been requested by the petitioners to seek an interview with the Secretary of State for the Colonies so that the Colonial Office could receive firsthand information on the causes of the disturbances and meet 'a true, faithful and worthy representative of the people of this island.' The organizers of the petition identified themselves in the document as Dan F. Blackett, H. Gordon Cummins, W.A. Crawford, James A. Tudor, and C.A. Brathwaite.

5   This account of the reasons for Adams's visit to England seems credible. Adams left Barbados on 6 September, but the petition which gave political legitimacy to that trip was organized *after* he left, and it was delivered to the governor on 23 September 1937.

6   Fabriciano Alexander (Sir Alexander) Hoyos (1912–2001), the biographer of Grantley Adams, published at least three books which deal with this period; and was the author of general histories of the island.

7   Christopher Augustus 'Chrissie' Brathwaite (1881–1952) was the durable link between the political activism of the 1920s and the movement for political democratization of the late 1930s and early 1940s. He was a founder member of O'Neal's Democratic League and represented the parish of St. Michael in the House of Assembly from 1924 to 1940.

8   Clennell Wilsden Wickham (1895–1938) was, along with O'Neal and 'Chrissie' Brathwaite, a pivotal figure in the political mobilisation of lower income groups during the 1920s. Through the columns of the *Herald*, which he edited, he offered incisive analyses of the prevailing social and political conditions, outlined a socialist agenda, and established himself, according to F.A. Hoyos, as 'the interpreter of the needs and aspirations of the underprivileged.'

CHAPTER 7

Formation of The Barbados Progressive League

he Progressive League was formed in 1938 shortly after the 1937 disturbances. There were a number of outstanding West Indians in America, In New York especially, and a few in Boston and Chicago, who always demonstrated the maximum interest in West Indian leaders. After the disturbances in St Vincent and St Kitts, Barbados, Trinidad and Jamaica and throughout the region, this group established the West Indies Defence Committee. On its Executive Committee were Hope Stevens, a barrister, Reginald Pierrepointe, a journalist, Dr Petioni, Richard Moore, whose library is now at Cave Hill, a Jamaican, W.A. Domingo, an Antiguan, A.A. Austin, and Mr Morris from Guyana.

That Committee was very vocal on West Indian affairs and it did two things. It collected money in New York and it sent Hope Stevens, who was born in Tortola and raised in St. Kitts-Nevis, to render some financial assistance to the Butler union in Trinidad. He also went to help a man who was in conflict with the authorities in Suriname for agitating workers.

He came to Barbados at the time that Grant was in prison after the riots and was asked to see me when he came in. He wanted to know what I thought was the most urgent issue in Barbados at that time or what I thought would contribute the greatest assistance in improving the situation. I told him that what I thought we needed most urgently was a movement in which all the progressive forces could be united, in order to present a common front and try to wrest power from the hands of the

J.A. Martineau

planter and mercantile barons. He said, 'Do you mean an organisation?' I said, 'Yes, that is precisely what I mean.' So it was decided that I would invite a few people to meet him on his return from Trinidad and Suriname. I invited a number of people and we met when he came back, in Bay Street, where one of the people I had invited, Mr J.A. Martineau, had a soft drinks plant. Martineau told me that he would like to have us at his house and that he would entertain us that night. At that meeting in Martineau's house, we decided to form a political organisation. The others present were 'Chrissie' Brathwaite, Martineau, Talma, Jack Ashby, Philip Payne and Hugh Cummins.[1] I believe that the Barbados Labour Party has published a little brochure with the names of the people who where there.[2]

Hope Stevens came to Barbados many years afterwards and told me one day, 'You know, there are only three remaining members who were

Martineau's House at corner of Bay and Beckwith Streets

Newspaper headline (Daily Nation, 13 January 1978)

in attendance that night: you and Edwy Talma and myself, and we should get together and give a press conference about the formation of the Labour Party' (as it was originally called). We did this, and the interview appeared in the *Nation* about five years ago. I recommended Chrissie Brathwaite as the first President because I figured that his years of service to the cause entitled him to that, and he was appointed. Adams was not in the island. He had gone to St Lucia in connection with legal action taken by Timothy Howell, a dentist, against *The St. Lucia Voice* published by George Gordon, Garnet Gordon's father. I recommended Adams as Vice-President of the organization. I was offered the post of Secretary, which I had to decline on the grounds that I had just started to publish the *Barbados Observer* and that it was such an uphill task that I could not possibly

H.G. Cummins

devote appropriate time to both. Talma was appointed to that post, and we started off from there. But most of the groundwork in the building up of the League (the Labour Party, as it was called) was done by a man called Herbert Seale.

The name of the organization was changed. It was first called the Barbados Labour Party. Subsequently, the name was changed. I understand that somebody said that it was too radical a name for an organization in Barbados at the time, and to call it the Labour Party would antagonize large numbers of middle class people who would not be associated with it at all. So the name was changed to the Progressive League.

My recollection is that it was returned to 'Labour Party' under the influence of Hugh Springer when they were preparing to fight my Congress Party in elections in the 1940s. This was largely due to the fact that Bustamante had swept the vote in Jamaica, defeating Manley with his Jamaica Labour Party. Bustamante had been released from jail to fight Norman Manley, who was fighting for self-government, and the British were naturally opposing him. Bustamante smashed Manley's party at the polls.

Herbert Seale was really the builder of the League. I met him when he came here. He was in business before he entered politics. He told me that he had been one of the forefront supporters of the Garvey movement and he had acquired a lot of platform oratory from his association with Marcus Garvey.

After I broke with the Progressive League, I warned Seale against associating with Grantley Adams and told him that, instead of joining the Progressive League, he should join me and start a party. He chose to go into the League. He and a man called Sydney 'Boysie' Skinner, whom I met in London some years afterwards, started holding meetings in the city and suburbs, night after night. When Seale left the League after a clash with Adams, the League had something like 27,000 members and $10,000 in the bank.

As the membership of the League grew, the workers were beginning to demand better conditions. A busman's strike took place and the men lost their jobs. Seale was blamed and as a result he resigned as Secretary of the League. The executive of the League held a meeting which Adams did not attend. Brathwaithe, Martineau and the rest of the committee proposed to give Seale an honorarium of $240.00 in recognition of his services to the organization. Adams did not agree and he used it as a tool for getting rid of the organization's leadership. He never told anybody in the organisation that he was going to call a meeting. He suddenly announced a meeting in Queen's Park at which he was to be the speaker. Nobody from the League was with him. When Adams got there, he saw a man called Barry Springer in the audience. He said to him, 'Barry, come and take this Chair for me,' and Barry said, 'Man, I never took a Chair in my life.' Adams said, 'Just sit down, I will tell you what to do.' Barry went and took the Chair. Adams then proceeded to lambaste Brathwaite and Martineau and that stirred up the crowd. He told them, 'Now imagine all this money you worked so hard for – all your hard earned pennies you have contributed to the League, and now they want to pick it up and give it to Herbert Seale.' He gave the impression they were giving away half the money when the amount was a mere $240.00. In recognition of what Barry did that night, Adams ran him afterwards in St Andrew and got him into the House for a year.

The next morning, when I went down to town and heard about the attack, I went to Chrissie Brathwaite's place in Roebuck Street and said, 'Chrissie, have you heard what happened?' He said, 'Yes, I heard.' I said, 'What are you going to do about it?' He said, 'Nobody will notice Adams. I am a respectable citizen. I have been in the House for years; I have been churchwarden and everybody knows me. I have been in the Vestry for years and nobody will believe that kind of tripe.' I said to him, 'Listen to me! From the way Adams put the matter over last night, everybody believes that you picked up nearly all that money out of the bank to give to Herbert Seale. I advise that you hold a meeting in the Park tonight and deny it.' He said, 'You are young and you will learn, nobody will notice Grantley Adams. Everybody knows what Grantley Adams is like.' I was in my twenties. So I rang Martineau and said, 'You heard what happened last night.' He said, 'Yes, I heard and rang 'Chrissie' and told him he should do something about it. He said he wasn't going to do anything. Nobody is noticing Grantley Adams with his lies and so on.' I rang Dr Storey, I rang everybody that day, and everybody thought it was an evil move but nothing was done.

The next morning after that meeting in Queen's Park, 'Chrissie' could not get into his store. There was a mob in front of the store in Roebuck Street which was about two or three buildings from where H.O. Emtage used to be. There was a big mob blocking the entrance and shouting, 'We want our money! Why are you using our money? You gave our money to Herbert Seale!' The crowd was so infuriated that he was probably afraid to go and hold a meeting. It would probably have got out of hand.

They all left the League immediately – Martineau, Cummins, 'Chrissie', Storey, everybody – and left it to Adams who took over. 'Chrissie' lost his seat that year. He had been in the House for many years and he was one of the most popular men in the island. Apart from the fact that he had been in the Vestry and the House, I had made him President of the Labour Party (Progressive League) because he had served so well. Adams took this fiction about Herbert Seale getting the money and used it to take control of the organization.

At that time, elections were held every year, and Seale entered the 1940 election campaign as an Independent candidate for one of the two seats for the City of Bridgetown, fighting against Sir Harold Austin (a business magnate) and H.A. Vaughan. It was a terrific struggle because of their powerful platform oratory. As a matter of fact, Seale's strength in the city took Austin and Vaughan by surprise. Seale had been very successful in building up the Progressive League in the city and was well-known and liked. He would have won one of the seats were it not for a surprising event in the campaign. Adams was bitterly opposed to both Seale and Vaughan. His hostility to Vaughan derived not only from Vaughan's association with Dr O'Neal but also from the election campaign in St Philip when he ran against Vaughan and split the vote allowing the white contestants to win.[3] Adams was hostile to Seale because he thought Seale was too ambitious and too popular and he was afraid of him. Adams seems to have supported Austin who in turn supported Vaughan. Austin told his supporters to vote for Vaughan along with himself, and that tide carried Vaughan and Austin in. Seale was left out.

Some time afterwards, Erskine Ward, who was then the Registrar, phoned to tell me that Seale was going to be arrested. When I asked him what for, he said, 'The workers loading coal on the waterfront are on strike.' In those days there was no deep water harbour and the ships that came in here mostly burnt coal, not oil. On the pierhead there was a coal bunker run by Laurie and Co. When the ships came in, a lot of women with baskets on their heads would go down there to load the coal in the lighters which would take the coal over to the ships. The war had started and emergency legislation had been enacted declaring all strikes illegal. That morning in question there were ships in the harbour to be 'coaled', but the women down there went on strike. They were getting an inordinately low wage for this work and it was an incredibly dirty job. On evenings when they finished work, you could not see them because the coal was all over their heads and faces and clothes. They decided not to work for that kind of money anymore because the price of coal had gone up tremendously. It was intimated to me that the Colonial Secretary called Grantley Adams to inquire what he knew about the strike and who had instigated it and that Grantley told him that it was Seale who had called it. This was not all true. Seale knew nothing about it, but the order went out to the Attorney General to arrest him.

I told Erskine I was not warning Seale. Ward's reply to me was, 'You can't do that, I believe he is innocent.' Seale was then running an agency almost a block from my *Observer* office at the corner of Prince William Henry Street. Eventually Erskine persuaded me to call him. So Seale came over to my office and I said, 'Look here, Herbert, there is a warrant out for your arrest.' He said 'What for?' I said, 'For this coal strike down on the wharf.' He said, 'I know nothing about that. I only just heard what was going on. Anyhow, I don't know what I can do.' Now his father was a planter, who owned the Rock Dundo plantation in St Michael. So he said, 'My father is a bit annoyed with me, but I will go and see him right away. He knows Keith Walcott, the Attorney General, very well.' So he went there and his father telephoned Keith Walcott, and said, 'Keith, I asked that boy of mine about the strike. He knows nothing about it. Although I don't agree with his politics, he doesn't tell lies. I believe him. He has nothing at all to do with it.' So Walcott told his father, 'Send him down to me right away.' He went down to the Attorney General's office and convinced him that he knew nothing at all about the strike. Years afterwards, in the 1960s, I met Sydney Skinner in London who told me, 'Mr. Crawford, I came to see you because I wanted to tell you, it is time somebody knew that Seale knew nothing at all about that strike.'

After this clash with the law, Seale got scared and left the island and went to New York. I think he is still alive. A lady who knew him well told me that she thought he was still alive in New York, in a nursing home. Somehow he developed a persecution complex after all he had gone through in Barbados, and I am told he was forever telling people that the FBI was after him.

Hilton Vaughan had been in the House for some time and at heart he was with the people. He could not understand why the masses turned to Adams who had joined with the Conservatives to attack O'Neal and himself when they were fighting in the people's interest. Vaughan fought like the devil during the Herbert Seale campaign. I went to a meeting in Queen's Park one night during the campaign and heard him attack a man who was supporting Seale. He really went down in the gutter and I expressed my surprise to Erskine Ward who was also there. He told me that I must understand that the people want to hear that you can defend yourself when you are attacked. If you cannot defend yourself, then they think you cannot defend them. That was intended to bring Vaughan back up and he did defeat Seale.

When I entered the House in 1940, Vaughan was still there but he was disillusioned. He could not understand how Herbert Seale nearly beat him. He sat beside me for that year and I am sure that often when Keith Walcott, the Attorney General, was dealing with some reactionary proposal or was saying something which needed defending, I would turn to Vaughan and say, 'Look here, don't let him get away with that. When he sits, we will fix him up'. Vaughan told me more than once, 'Me, man I am not saying one single word. If the masses want Adams, let them have him.' At the end of the year, he took a job as magistrate.

I think that Adams switched from being a professional or careerist and chose a life in politics because he was flabbergasted at the following Payne picked up in a short time and the strength which the new labour movement gave him. Adams had ignored it before. He used to pooh-pooh O'Neal but he grabbed the opportunity when he saw it. In addition, he was forty and more experienced than most of his opponents. Adams was a very skilful fellow. They used to call him Sir John Simon after the distinguished English barrister and Liberal politician. I had heard Brancker say repeatedly that Adams modelled his career on Sir John Simon. People switch. Churchill switched more than once.

Notes

1   James Augustus Martineau (1892–1969) was a businessman who, like James A. Tudor, was a supporter of the progressive cause. He served in the St. Michael Vestry from 1935 to 1940. Cuthbert Edwy (Sir Edwy) Talma (1909–1994) is an illustration of the fluidity of political party lines in the 1940s and 1950s. A founder member of the Progressive League (the Barbados Labour Party) in 1938, he was a member of Crawford's Congress Party in 1944–1947, returned to the Barbados Labour Party in 1947, and ended his political career with the Democratic Labour Party in the 1970s. Dr Hugh Gordon Cummins (1892–1970) was a long-standing progressive politician. He contested elections for the House of Assembly under the Democratic League's banner in 1925, represented the parish of St. Thomas in the Assembly from 1935–36 and from 1940 to 1961, and was Premier of Barbados from 1958 to 1961, when Sir Grantley Adams became Prime Minister of the Federation of the West Indies.

2   Other accounts of that historic meeting do not mention the name Jack Ashby.

3   Hilton Augustus Vaughan (1901–1985), lawyer, poet, historian, was a supporter of liberal causes. He served in the House of Assembly as the representative of Bridgetown from 1936 to 1940 when he accepted a judgeship. He returned to politics in 1961 when he was appointed to the Legislative Council and to the post of Attorney General in the first Barrow Cabinet.

CHAPTER 8

Active Politician and Party Leader

In 1939, before the war started, I was kept until 2.00 a.m. one morning at Grantley Adams's house with him and his wife encouraging me to run for the City against H.A. Vaughan. When I refused, I was told: 'You bound to get in because people who don't know you know the *Barbados Observer* and, if you run, you are bound to get the seat.' I refused to run against Hilton Vaughan, and I had not quite decided to run the following year either. But then the war started and there was some talk about elections being postponed, as in England, until after the war was finished. So I decided that I had better run in 1940 if I wanted to get in because I did not know how long the war would last.

I actually started campaigning in St. George. The sitting members were E.S. Robinson, one of the largest sugar industrialists in the country, and Charlie Elder. My family did not want me to run in St. George because they were friendly with Charlie Elder but I said, 'There are two seats and I know I could probably get one.' So I began canvassing up there, and I had a lot of support from people all over the parish. One man who gave me a lot of support was the Headmaster of St Jude's School, Mr Clyde Barrow. Support also came from Mr Goring and a prominent blacksmith and two brothers who had big groceries.

Sir Hugh Springer

I was going very well in St George and then, one Saturday morning, Hugh Springer walked into my newspaper office and said to me, 'I am very sorry; Grantley Adams wants me to run in St George. We had a meeting of the League last night to select candidates for the general election and Adams nominated me for St. George. I told him that you were already running and he said, "Well, if you do not want to run, I will have to nominate somebody else. But we running a man in St. George." I am very, very sorry, but you know I didn't have any other alternative. I have to run because I was nominated.'[1] This was late in the year, perhaps early December. So I said 'Well, I'll tell you something; I was there before you and I will not leave. Neither of us will get in because we are going to cut the progressive votes (a small number of votes) and put Elder and Robinson back in.' He said, 'I can easily see that myself.' So I went back to the parish and began telling my supporters what had happened, and they said, 'Crawf, you were here before so we will simply give you our support.'

A few years before, when Adams and Vaughan had run in St Philip, they had split the progressive vote and put back in the two conservative planters, Dr Hawkins and E.B. Skeete. So I remember very well on New Year's Day saying to myself, 'You know something, if they postpone elections until after the war, you might be out of politics for another five years, or as long as the war lasts'. So I drove to St Philip to where King George V Park is now. I saw a man grazing a cow. I stopped to talk to him and began questioning him about the election candidates for the parish. He said, 'Well, you know we've got Dr Hawkins.' Hawkins was a doctor and he owned Foursquare sugar factory in addition to four or five estates totalling over 2,000 acres in St Philip. He said, 'We also have a man called Lisle Smith. (He was another big sugar industrialist whose family controlled a number of plantations and sugar factories.) He has gone to the war but Mr Skeete from either Bentley or Edgecumbe plantations is contesting the seat, and also Major Peebles.' Peebles was a retired British colonial administrator whom I had met before in St Vincent. He came here and married into a wealthy Barbadian family, the Camerons, also representatives of the sugar plantocracy. So I said to myself, 'If I want to get in now, I had better switch because, if I remain in St George, I am not going to get in with Springer running and he will not get in either. And if I leave and go to St Philip, there is every possibility both he and I would get in.' So I left St George and went to St Philip just about a couple of months before the elections.

The first thing I decided to do, although I was late, was to start registering people up there. There were numbers to be registered. I used to take up a friend called Jack Ashby who was a J.P., 'Chrissie' Brathwaite and, sometimes, Brancker.[2] We would meet at night and we would register people. And then, to my surprise, just before the elections, the registering officer refused to have those people registered on the voters' list. He said they were too late. I wrote an article in the *Barbados Observer* accusing him of improper discharge of his responsibilities, and he promptly threatened to sue me for libel.

In those days in a libel action, you had no chance at all because all your opponents had to do was to employ a Special Jury, as Bayley had done against Clennell Wickham. If one applied for a Special Jury, it was granted automatically. I could not fight it, so I had to withdraw the statement, and he made me pay a small amount towards the war effort, and the people I had registered could not vote at that election. Peebles, who was running against me, was reported to be fairly liberal in his way. Yet, he was a newcomer to Barbados and there was no reason at all why he would have a claim on the people of St Philip for their support. In addition, he was associated with the planter class which had been responsible for the depression and the economic difficulties of the working classes.

I myself had no ties with the parish either. Apart from my identification with the interests of the working class, I was a stranger to the parish. In the course of the campaign, I had a clash with an Englishman, Rev Stanton, who was the Rector of St Philip Parish Church. He organized a campaign against my election and held a meeting in the St George's Parish Church with some of the other Anglican parsons from St Philip. He told them that I had no right coming into the parish, that I wanted to oppose people who owned plantations and sugar factories, and that kind of thing. He asked the ministers in the various churches to campaign against me.

Then a friend told me that this man was one of the Barnardo boys from England. He had been sent down here from London and eventually he went to Codrington College. After he was ordained, he had married the daughter of a very influential man in the church and had got a rectory.

Sir Theodore Brancker

I promptly called a meeting the following night, not too far from the church, and lambasted him, pointing out that he had owned nothing in the parish either. He never bothered me after that.

The Saturday night before the elections, Brancker and I were going through the parish to-gether, and everywhere we went we were told that my political opponent, Adams, had been running through the parish with Major Peebles, of all people, asking voters to support Peebles and not me. Theodore Brancker left me that night very dejected. He said, 'Crawf, you had the seat but I do not think you can make it now because there are only so many votes and even fifteen or twenty votes can throw you out.' So I said, 'You don't bother, Brancker, you leave it to me. I will fix him up.' So I went home, and the next morning, which was Sunday, I went down to town and got two of my printers from the *Observer* and told them I wanted some posters printed with the words – '**ADAMS NEEDS HELP. VOTE FOR CRAWFORD**'

Because Adams was moving around St Philip among the masses, I decided to sleep in the parish that night at a friend's house. I took a man with me called Darnley Greenidge and the next morning I woke him up early and said, 'You go and stick these posters all over the church walls, near the polling booth.' Voting was in the St Philip Parish Church.

He stuck the posters on the church walls and on the houses around. When the people came to vote, they said, 'Hey, Mr Adams telling us not to vote for Mr Crawford and here it is that Mr Crawford saying he is going into the House to help him. We are going to vote for Crawford. Don't mind Adams.' Since then, I have heard a lot of people repeating the story that I used a poster with Adams's name on it – but I would never have thought about doing it at all if Adams had not been canvassing against me.

In those days it was a very difficult thing for an outsider to get a seat because, apart from the small number of electors, you had to have the qualification of a small salary or property before you could become a candidate or a voter. The smallholders were in the position that, if they did not vote, or if it was thought that they had not voted for the factory owner, he would not lend them money between crops to get manure and labour; or, when the factory started to grind canes, he would not accept their canes. One of the most important hardships was that, before the grinding season started, most of these smallholders were highly indebted to the sugar factory owners for loans and manure.

One of the first promises of my campaign was that, if I were elected, I would see to it that the government established a loan bank for all the smallholders, which would operate in the same way the Sugar Industry Bank operated for the big planters and factory owners. Despite the fact that none of the men we had registered was allowed to vote at all, I still won a seat by a handsome margin.[3]

I had been active among the peasant farmers, and the most important incident which persuaded me to start a party was related to the agricultural workers. I also realized that more members with similar ideas had to be brought into the House of Assembly if our programme was to be put through. As a result of making the sugar workers' strike a major issue, I was able to start the West Indian National Congress Party. Some of my early colleagues were Brancker, Hugh Blackman, Dr John Wilson, Edwy Talma and D.D. Garner. The grievances of the cane cutters led to a big agricultural strike in 1944–45 and provided the first opportunity for some reform.

Newspaper Headline

Nowadays we have furrows but in those days the land was cultivated in cane holes, about 1,600 holes to the acre. The canes were planted in these holes which were probably about two-and-a-half feet square and about ten inches in depth, and when it came to harvesting, the workers were paid for cutting canes by the hundred holes.

I went to my constituency in St Philip one afternoon, to a village behind Ebenezer, and in conversation with a few chaps who came down from Church Village, it was drawn to my attention that cane-cutters and agricultural workers, not only in St Philip but throughout the island, were dissatisfied with the manner in which they were being paid for cutting canes. In some parts of St Philip bordering Christ Church where the rainfall was limited and the land not as fertile, the yield of canes was fifteen to twenty tons to the acre. But, in other parts of St Philip bordering St George and St John, the yield was forty to sixty tons to the acre because of the higher rainfall and more fertile land. It might take three or four days to cut a hundred holes in a high rainfall area and less than a day in a low rainfall area, yet the pay would be the same 36 cents. It appeared to me to be the most dishonest thing that I had heard in all my life and I said that something had to be done about it.[4]

So I went on tour of the island myself. I went to St Joseph, St Thomas, St Lucy, St Peter, and everywhere, I found that this problem was a bone of contention. So I discussed it with my colleagues – Theodore Brancker, Hugh Blackman, retired Assistant Postmaster General at the time, Dr John Wilson, the eye specialist, Edwy Talma, D.D. Garner and others and got them to agree that something should be done about this injustice. We called a meeting upstairs a building in High Street where Mr C.N. Weekes had a canteen and invited all the agricultural workers to come in on the Monday morning that the crop was supposed to start to discuss the matter. The response was overwhelming.

We had previously held a number of meetings throughout the island telling people that it was criminal that they should cut canes by the hundred holes and that we were prepared to back them to the hilt in order to get it changed. On the morning the crop was supposed to start, workers from every parish poured into Bridgetown into our place in High Street. There were about six of us up on the platform. There was a lady there, too, who later became the wife of Sir Erskine Ward. At one time we were nearly pushed off the platform out into the street because of the crowd. So we decided it was impossible to carry on there. I suggested that we march to Queen's Park and hold the meeting there. So we vacated the building and we led the march from High Street up to Queen's Park with all the agricultural workers behind us. Many of them had their cane bills, and the merchants in Broad Street got scared stiff and shut their doors immediately.

There were thousands of people there. All my colleagues and myself insisted that the workers should not cut a single blade until the system was changed. We caused a general strike throughout the industry. No factory could start at all, and the strike went on week after week. We held meetings right through and begged the shopkeepers to credit the workers with goods until such time as the crop started, because we were sure that we could win and that they could get their money back. One thing I must say is that the small shopkeepers throughout the island responded admirably.

There were numerous cane fires. We were accused of telling the workers to start the fires but we knew that it was not the workers who were responsible. It was the planters who were setting fires to the canes because they were insured. As a matter of fact, the police actually caught Keith Weatherhead, a white overseer at Sandy Lane Plantation, setting fire to a cane field. All the newspapers including my own reported it. He got Grantley Adams to go into court with him, and Adams got him off. I was informed that, some years afterwards, the same young man committed suicide. He went up to Dover Beach and blew his head off.

I do not remember exactly how many weeks the strike lasted.[5] We were insisting at the meetings that the government bring in an independent arbitrator from outside to settle the issue. On the floor of the House I tabled a resolution to that effect. At this time, Adams's party was holding meetings telling the people to cut the canes; that they could not get the system changed; nor could they get the $1.00 per hundred holes we were demanding as a minimum. The people did not notice them at all.

Eventually, the government, in response to our insistent demand, brought in Professor C.Y. Shephard from the Imperial College of Tropical Agriculture (ICTA) in Trinidad as arbitrator. He went through the entire issue with us and with the planters, and presented a report to the government completely endorsing our position with a recommendation that the canes should be cut by the ton. The government and the planters had to agree and, from then until now, canes are cut by the ton. Our position was further justified when, in the formula that Professor Shephard gave the government for a price for cutting canes in the areas of heavy agricultural yields, the workers got more than $1.00 per hundred holes. Nobody got less than $1.00.

There were many other problems affecting agriculture. These included the price paid for peasants' canes; the manner in which they were weighed when they went on the factory scales; and the importance of rendering financial assistance in the early parts of the year after the crop to peasants and agricultural workers who rented land from the estates. We finally got the Agricultural Credit Bank started (1961) to deal with the matter of financing the peasants.

In 1943, the first Labour Commissioner, Guy Perrin, had been appointed. He set up three councils in different parts of the island in which representatives of sugar workers from each district met the planters in the sugar industry to discuss conditions of work every year before the crop started. I immediately offered my services to join the council that included my constituency while Adams and Springer offered to serve on the other two. George Lamming once told me that he was doing some assignments for the Workers' Union and he wanted to have an interview with me because wherever he went throughout the island in the sugar districts and asked the workers about people who contributed to their improvement, he always met with the name 'Crawford.'

I went to St Philip one day with Perrin, to show him the conditions at Foursquare factory. In those days, during almost every crop, people would get killed because of poor safety conditions for workers, and when I showed Perrin Foursquare, he could not believe that the factory's management would expose machinery like that to injure people. Since then (in 1948, 1982), we have had legislation introduced in Barbados, compelling factory supervisors to see about the safety conditions of the workers.

In the election of 1944 the Congress Party got eight seats, one-third of the total number of seats. However, there was a dispute about whether I should be on the Executive Committee. Adams chose Hugh Springer, and with the agreement of the Governor they decided to form a coalition with the Conservatives who had also got eight seats. J.H. Wilkinson and Stanley Robinson from Constant were their two representatives along with Adams and Springer on the Executive Committee.[6]

In spite of this, I devoted a considerable amount of time to affairs in St Philip, my constituency. The agricultural workers had many grievances. There was the Located Labourers Act which required labourers to work for a certain number of days every week on a particular plantation even when they could obtain work for higher wages on another estate. It was obvious that they needed some kind of organization to represent them, so we started a union, the Congress Union, for agricultural workers, but neither of the two men we had doing the office work was really a good organizer. At the same time, we were very busy trying to organize the Party, holding meetings everywhere. You see, in those days there were no loudspeakers and you had to organize meetings in small districts and talk to people. You could not get before a mike and broadcast.

The treasurer of the union was Hugh Blackman who was a retired civil servant, and there was another very committed helper called Simeon but he needed training. It was an unpaid job and the wages of the workers were so low that they could not afford to pay the union contributions. It was easier to organize the urban workers, especially the waterfront workers, because they worked for much higher wages.

The waterfront workers were the backbone of unionization for a long time. I think that after Adams decided to go into politics he realised that it had to be a full-time job. I could not do it because I had to work for a living. It was the urban workers in the Barbados Workers' Union who paid Adams his salary. It was easier to represent them because every time they wanted an increase they got it. You see, the port had to be kept working all the time so, if they said they wanted a certain wage, it was paid to them after a little struggle, and then the additional costs would be put on the price of goods.

Low wages as well as seasonal employment in the rural districts made it difficult to organize the agricultural workers. We had two or three organizers in different districts working, and they would come in and say that they could not collect dues from a lot of people. Then you needed to get transportation because when they had grievances on an estate down in St Andrew or St Lucy or elsewhere, you had to send a man out there. We could not afford to pay somebody and provide a car or provide the necessary support. It was a difficult job, so the union did not last.

When I was first elected, I made some tours through the districts of St. Philip so that I could see conditions for myself. One day I went up to the police station at District C and met the Sergeant. I said, 'Sergeant, what are things like up here? Are there any complaints? What are the conditions under which the men work up here?' He said to me, 'Mr. Crawford, you see that cart there with the animals in front of us? Do you know what it is for? There is no running water in the police station at all. The police who live here, myself, the magistrate, people who come to court, the lawyers and everybody – they want water. Every drop of water used in this station is brought here from a pipe at the bottom of the hill by that mule and cart in those two barrels you see there. There is a tank, and when the rain falls, we would get a little too.' I could not believe it. No running water at all in a police station! So, the following Tuesday, I tabled a Resolution in the House of Assembly drawing attention to the situation and insisting that the place be given running water immediately. After that, I made it my business to see that there was running water in every nook and cranny in the parish. Before that, no district – not even Brereton, Edgecumbe or Church Village – had water. As a matter of fact, there was only one district in Church Village, called Cottage Vale, which had water. In upper Church Village at the top of the hill, there is a place called Cliff Lane on the border of St John. People had to walk down a long hill about two miles to get water from the bottom of that hill. Then in the eastern part of the parish, Ruby and the Ruby district – everywhere that water was needed – I had it installed.

Similarly with electricity; in my last term of office (1961–1965), I had the final stage of electricity installed. This included Foul Bay, the St Martin's area, right through to the eastern part of the parish to East Point and back down. The parish had roads and water. Everything was done to improve the basic amenities.

It was through a man called Catlyn that I became aware of the plight of the fishermen in Foul Bay. When they came in with the catch of fish in the boats, they had to climb a hill which was a hell of a steep climb. The fishermen used to put the fish around their necks with a string and climb up the hill with them, and sell to the hawkers on the plateau. I promised Catlyn to see what I could do. On the next Vestry nomination day, I went into the Vestry room at St Philip's Boys' School and I told the Vestrymen that it was not fair at all that the fishermen in that district should have so much trouble to get their catch up to sell. A road was needed there and they should put some money in the estimates for the preparation of a road or get some money from the central government. As a result, a road was cut so that the fishermen could have easy access up and the women could buy the fish. At East Point, in the area formerly called Windy Ridge, I also had a road cut down to the beach and had water installed so that when the fishermen came up out of the sea they could get fresh water. It is a beautiful road. Those two roads I will never forget. I also had them repair the Market Road which had been closed for ninety-nine years. People complained to me, especially during the crop, about getting to Foursquare or Oldbury sugar factories. So I persuaded the Vestry to open up that road.

I had also made the government clear a place called Megs Channel. There is a coral reef around the eastern part of Barbados, right around the

Crane and Foul Bay to Sam Lord's Castle. The boats fishing off the Crane had to go through a channel to get out to sea. Apparently, the coral reef had grown and blocked the entire channel, and the men could not go out there for fear of being capsized. So I went to the floor of the Assembly with a resolution calling on the government immediately to get the channel cleared so that these people could make a living. I suggested that the thing to do was to dynamite it. There was a furore in the House with members claiming, 'if you dynamite that channel, the water would come in and take over a part of the parish.' They said I wanted to drown the island, and all sorts of things. I insisted that the government bring in fishery experts to check it. The government got a fishery expert from Trinidad, a man called Brown, who immediately said the thing to do was to dynamite it. So they dynamited the channel, and the boats were able to go out again.

In the meantime, there had been an island-wide interest in the matter. A Mr Shepherd, a boat owner who lived near St Aidan's church in Bathsheba, invited me to come down to Tent Bay near the Atlantis Hotel to see the fishing boats come in. They came in at odd hours between 2.00 p.m. and 6.00 p.m., and those fishermen who came in first were unable to leave the beach because they had to wait to help the other boats come in through the narrow channel. I told Mr Shepherd that I did not represent St Joseph but he insisted that I should help them too. They needed a winch to help haul up the boats. I said, 'Well, I don't represent the parish

Fishing Boats at Tent Bay, Bathsheba, St. Joseph

but what I can do is to arrange for the Governor, Sir Grattan Bushe, and the Fishery Officer to come down here and see this thing for themselves.' In the meantime, I arranged to take Shepherd and another fisherman to Government House myself to talk to the Governor about it. Incidentally, once our Congress Party wanted to take some agricultural workers to Government House, some Labour Party people raised hell about it, saying we were taking ordinary people to Government House.

I took the two men to see Sir Grattan Bushe who listened to what we had to say, after which we invited him to come down to Bathsheba to see the situation for himself. We had refreshments at the Atlantis Hotel and remained to watch the fishing boats come in. He promised the fishermen faithfully that, as soon as the war was over, he would try and get that winch for them. Shortly after the war ended, they got the winch and had it installed to haul up the boats at Tent Bay. The building which houses it has a light at the corner and that light is directly opposite to the channel at Tent Bay where the boats come through. When the fishermen come in late, all they have to do is to put the bow of the boat straight on that light and come safely through the channel.

It actually saved my life once. One evening, 'Cow' Williams who had a fishing boat said to me, 'Barracudas biting off Codrington College like the devil, man. Come down and I will take you fishing.' I liked fishing. so I went down and took Captain Kidd, husband of the Hon Janet Kidd of Holders, John Defreitas from the poultry farm at Montrose, and another friend. We left early and went down almost to East Point lighthouse and came back in late when it was dark. We did not get back into Tent Bay until it was very, very black. But, fortunately, that light was on the building there, and 'Cow' Williams steered the boat directly for the light and came flying through the channel at about 8.00 p.m.

Notes

[1] Hugh Worrell (Sir Hugh) Springer (1913–1994), National Hero of Barbados, was Grantley Adams's principal lieutenant in the Barbados Labour Party and in the Barbados Workers' Union until 1947 when he joined the University College of the West Indies as its first Registrar. He represented the parish of St. George in the House of Assembly from 1940 to 1947.

2 John Eustace Theodore (Sir Theodore) Brancker (1909–1996), lawyer, was active in politics on the progressive side from the 1930s, and was successively a member of the Progressive League, the Congress Party, and the Democratic Labour Party. He represented the parish of St. Lucy from 1937 to 1971.

3   The St Philip parish, like the other eleven constituencies, was a double member constituency until 1971. In the 1940 election, Crawford polled 119 votes and Dr. Hawkins received 111 votes while the two losing candidates, R.B. Skeete and Major Peebles, received 104 and 80 votes respectively. Hugh Springer had a more impressive victory in St George. He polled 210 votes to 162 for E.S. Robinson and 148 for C.L. Elder.

4   The issue was perhaps slightly more complicated than Crawford remembers. Since 1939, cane cutters had been paid on a sliding scale: the rate for cutting 100 holes varied for each field according to the yield per acre. In other words, the higher the yield per acre, the higher the wage for cutting 100 holes. What the representatives of the cane cutters demanded in 1944/45 was a flat and increased rate for cutting 100 holes; but the employers insisted on paying on the sliding scale.

5   The strike, which was never comprehensive, lasted at least two months – from February to April 1945 – with the result that the crop finished in August, more than two months after the end of the normal grinding season. The losses to the industry, from the work stoppage, cane fires and extension of the grinding season beyond the optimal period, were staggering: a reduction of at least 30,000 tons in output and loss of national income of about two million dollars.

6   Until semi-responsible government came to Barbados with the Bushe Experiment in 1946, the Governor was not constitutionally bound to respect the wishes of the electorate in his choice of members of the Executive Committee. However, after the impressive performance of the Congress Party in its first elections, the Governor told the Secretary of State for Colonies that he would have liked to appoint a member of that party to the Executive Committee 'but I regret to say that there is no member of that party whom I could at present consider having on the Executive Committee.'

CHAPTER 9

The Cut And Thrust Of Party Politics

Owen T. Allder did not start his political career with the Barbados Labour Party. The Congress Party ran Allder in a by-election in St Peter in 1945, the year that James Ramsay resigned. I personally did not think he could get in. He seemed too immature, but we tried to get some support for him anyhow, and Hugh Blackman, treasurer of the Party, and Winnie Wharton were supporting him. During the campaign he came to me and complained that one of the party leaders was telling the people in St Peter that, rather than vote for him, vote for 'Jubie' Reece. I told him that I had heard it also.

I nearly got killed during the campaign that year. One day I found myself alone quite far down in the back of the buildings where we were campaigning. It was around 1:00 p.m. or 2:00 p.m. I was really looking for somewhere private to urinate. When I was coming back up, I saw three men, not too far away. One turned out to be a man from St Joseph, who was a very strong supporter of the Labour Party. His name was Fields Lowe. I was going towards the three men and suddenly Lowe said, 'Hey, hey, look Crawford down there, man. Look Crawford down there by himself with nobody at all; leh we kill him down here today. He is our big opponent.' I was scared but I decided the best thing to do was to put on a brave front because it would have been one against three and there was nobody else around there at all. He was ahead of the other fellows, so I decided to put up a fight. I said, 'Fields, let me tell you something; the two

of them might kill me but, before they kill me, I will tear your guts out.'
So in the heat of the moment I put my head down and started running
straight between his legs. I knew he had a hydrocele. He got scared and
started reversing and the others went back too. That is perhaps the only
thing that saved my life that day.

Political campaigning was becoming more turbulent and sometimes
we had a little violence. I remember once we were organising peasants to
get a good price and proper weights for their sugar cane on the factory
scales. We organised a meeting in St Joseph. Three or four of them were
to start this meeting about 6:00 p.m. When we got down to St Joseph for
the meeting and I saw the location, I could not believe it. When I organised
a public meeting, I always had a building at my back. But they were in the
midst of a cane field. I said, 'Man, you can't hold a meeting here. It is
impossible. You cannot see what is coming from behind in a cane field.'
As soon as they tried to talk, a lot of bottles and stones were thrown by
opposition supporters from the cane fields, and they had to stop. I paid
them back for it though, because when Adams came to St Philip to have
a meeting at Four Roads, we put up our equipment just across the road,
and they could not talk at all.

One night we had a meeting at Welchman Hall, St Thomas, near
Welchman Hall Gully. A man named Barnett lived in a house at the
corner. We were speaking from the platform of a lorry and, about an hour
after the meeting started, another lorry drew up with some men on it, but
I did not pay them any mind. Two of the men came and said they wanted
to have a little chat with me about something very important, and asked
if we could get away from the noise. So we started to go down to the top
of the gully. I got a bit apprehensive and said, 'Look, we can talk here.'
They said that, because of the noise of the loud speaker, we should go a
little further down. I said, 'No, we won't, we are turning back right here.'
Just at that time, Mr. Barnett came out and called me and said, 'Mr.
Crawford, I saw you with those two men and I was very scared because
those two men only left Glendairy (prison) yesterday and were brought
up here to see what confusion they could create.' This was sometime in
the 1940s.

Years later, when Erskine Ward and I held a meeting in Queen's Park
(after we broke from the Democratic Labour Party), there was a real threat
of violence when stones and bottles were thrown. People thought there
might be trouble and they were scared to death. Normally, I would say (I
mean, these are my personal experiences) that we did not have a lot of
the violence as did Jamaica, but still one had to be careful.

In the election campaign of 1946 I had just returned from Panama and I remember leaving St Philip, my constituency, on election day and driving to the city to help 'T.T.' Lewis who was the candidate running for the Congress Party. I spent a couple of hours down there trying to round up voters and talking to people. When I left there, Lewis had actually started to cry, saying he could not get in. I said to him, 'No, man, I think you've got it made, 'T.T', don't give up.' I left later in the afternoon feeling fairly sure he was in, and I went to St John where we had Hugh Blackman and Dr Wilson running.

'T.T.' Lewis won the seat. At the very first meeting of the House of Assembly after the election, when a Congress Party member, Dr Wilson, proposed something in connection with American emigration, 'T.T' got up and opposed it, to the utter surprise of everybody in the Assembly. The lady who is now Lady Ward came to me outside and asked me if Lewis knew what he was doing. Then 'T.T' Lewis came to me and said, 'Man, Crawford, the position is this. You all are not contesting in the urban areas, you all are in the country districts, and here in the city of Bridgetown Adams has the waterfront workers tied up in the Union. They have the hand-cart men in the Union and they are the fiercest opposition I have. This is the city of Bridgetown where the League is strong, so I got to work with Adams.' So I said, 'T.T.', I am surprised at you. Well, if you think that is what you should do, do it. It is a matter for you.'

After that, he was supposed to be working with Adams and, to my complete surprise, in 1952, Adams called a meeting in Queen's Park and invited Lewis to appear on the platform with him. I gathered that Adams lambasted him there. I was not at the meeting; I just heard what happened but I never really knew why Adams did it. 'T.T' was no longer with them after that meeting.

What I do know is that shortly after the election in 1946, my telephone at the newspaper office rang one day and the caller said, 'I am Mr. C.H. Kinch. Do you know me'? I said, 'Well, I have never met you, Mr Kinch, but I have heard of you.' Everybody had heard of Kinch who was a merchant in the city. I think he had a big trade with Canada and used to import most of the cod fish and flour and other Canadian goods that came into the island from a firm called W.S. Munroe, a big Canadian firm which later established itself here and remained in business for over 50 years.

He had a beautiful house at Worthing called Morecambe. There is a gasoline station in front of it now. He said, 'Since my wife died, I am not living in my house anymore. I now have a room at the Hotel Royal. You pass there every day to go home to Christ Church. I would like you to drop in to see me some time when you are passing by the hotel.' So, one evening on my way home, I dropped in at the hotel and was taken upstairs to see him, and he said to me, 'Mr Crawford, what I called you for was to tell you thanks very much for getting 'T.T' Lewis back in.' I said, 'What?' He said, 'Yes, I understand that you were very instrumental in getting him back into the House of Assembly again and I want to thank you for it.' I said, 'Mr Kinch, why should you thank me for that'? He said, 'Well, don't you know that he is one of our men?' Kinch was a white man and Lewis was white too. But Lewis had always, as far as we knew, been on the side of labour. I said, 'How would I know that, Mr Kinch? He ran with me in the Congress Party, and I couldn't think that he was one of your men too.' I do not know what Adams had heard, but Lewis had always appeared to be very progressive and to be one of us. But Kinch had me shocked. However, Lewis had already told me he was leaving me to go with Adams, so it was not really any of my business anymore.[1]

Subsequently, Lewis and Errol Barrow got very friendly, and Lewis ran with the DLP in the elections in 1956. I had joined them also and we were going great guns in that campaign. The parties were running neck and neck. Shortly before the elections, Barrow had suggested that we hold a meeting right outside Government House at the very top of Belmont Road, just at the top of Carrington Village. He said, 'There are a number of suggestions I am making.' That night Barrow got up and said that, if the DLP won the elections, we intended to put two masons, two carpenters, two waterfront workers and two longshoremen on the Legislative Council, which was the second chamber approximating to the British House of Lords. While he was talking, 'T.T' Lewis came to me and said, 'Oh my God, Crawford, pull that damn fool down. He is throwing away the election. He never discussed that with us. We never told him to say so.' So I said, 'T.T'. he has already said it. To go and contradict it now would make it worse.'

The majority opinion was that the speech threw away the election for us in 1956. On the Sunday before elections, what Barrow had said was rehashed in the newspaper by 'Mitchie' Hewitt, a journalist from the *Advocate* and, as a result, Barrow lost his seat the next day. There were only four of us left in the Party. 'Sleepy' Smith got in on the Adams ticket and then shortly afterwards crossed the floor and joined us. So I think that, if my mind serves me correctly, 'T.T' must have been a candidate in that 1956 election for the DLP. But after, that I do not think he ran again. He was not a candidate in the 1961 elections. But we all remained fairly friendly afterwards. I do not think he made any important contribution to political life in Barbados. There is nothing that I can say that he can be remembered by. He was, as Hoyos says, 'Meticulous for having commas in the correct places.' The fact that he was a white man who seemed to be on the side of the progressive forces made it possible for him to be elected.[2] In a minor manner this might have helped to break down the racial divisions that existed in the party. His wife was a mulatto girl from Dominica. In those days I suppose that might have had some little effect on the society. But he was a very friendly person and we all got along well with him.

He died quite young. I think he had a heart condition. He had a couple of children, but I do not know what became of them. They must have been brought up in St Lucia or Dominica. I would say that his contribution was more symbolic than anything else in the sense that he was a white man clearly identifying himself with the coloureds – not that it carried any special weight. You see, with the introduction of the party system, there was no longer the necessity to make individual contributions before one went into Parliament. It was always felt by some that he must have been a spent force by the time he reached the Assembly.

Apparently 'T.T' was a member of the Liberal Association of which H.A. Vaughan was a very prominent member. I remember that the Liberal Association was launched by a man called T. Archer McKenzie. It was in fact a political party. I heard about it but I knew it could never get off the ground because nobody had any confidence in McKenzie. He had no political base. He did not know where he was. Few seem to know anything about his politics. When I first knew McKenzie, I was a very young chap and he had a little store. He lived in Bay Street opposite the Hospital where the Child Care Board is now. He lost his store and he never recovered himself financially after that, as far as I know.

Personally, I never knew that H.A. Vaughan had any connection with the Liberal Association. My first intimation that Vaughan was connected with it was when, some years ago, I saw a magazine in the University in which there was mention of an article written by Tom Adams. It might have been a reply to some article by Vaughan, and it was lambasting Vaughan. It also had this information about Vaughan and the Liberal Association. So I rang Vaughan and said, 'Vaughan, have you seen that article in the University library in which Tom is giving you a slanging?' He said, 'No, I haven't seen it and I don't want to read it.' I said, 'Well, you should. It should be corrected because it isn't true. It is something about you and the Liberal Party.' Vaughan said to me (this is the first time that I was going to hear or realize that Vaughan was connected with the party), 'You know these people don't understand what we meant by the Liberal Party.'

Apparently, after it was started, Grantley Adams attacked it at a meeting in Queen's Park. Vaughan said to me, 'These people made the mistake of thinking that the Liberal Party was in the tradition of the Lloyd George or the Asquithian Liberal Party in England which was superseded by the Labour Party, but the Liberal Party I had in mind was more in the Prescodian sense – Samuel Jackman Prescod, but they don't know anything about that.' He dismissed it. So I never discussed it with him after that. You could not get Vaughan to protect himself at all. He just went back into his shell.

The Liberal Party was not properly launched. It would have been difficult for McKenzie to get a crowd to hear him anyhow, and Vaughan was not connected with it in the public's mind because his name was not mentioned anywhere in any prospectus or anything. People therefore only associated it with McKenzie, but I understood that McKenzie always used to be in Vaughan's office afterwards. Adams had probably heard about it and he connected Vaughan with it. He blasted him by saying he was putting the clock back fifty years.

This Liberal Party must have been started after the riots, and Vaughan disappeared from politics in 1941. Therefore I do not think that it would have come up after that. He became a magistrate and he would not have allowed himself to be formally associated with political parties.[3]

After the 1946 election, the West Indian National Congress had seven seats. The conservatives and Grantley Adams's party, the Progressive League, had an almost equal number of seats.[4] In the 1944–46 session Grantley Adams and Hugh Springer had represented their party on the Executive Committee along with two members of the conservative party, and my group in the Assembly had formed the opposition. Now, when the election results were declared, the conservatives were headed by J.H. Wilkinson, one of the biggest merchants and industrialist/planter-barons in the city, and by E.K. Walcott, the Attorney General. They immediately sent a message by J.E.T. Brancker to me suggesting that we should form a coalition. They invited me to a meeting at Brancker's house in St James to discuss the possibilities. At the meeting, Mr Wilkinson said to me, 'Mr Crawford, we're divided in three. We're three parties that the country has returned. We

Newspaper Headline

worked with Adams and Springer on the Executive Committee to run the country last session. Under no condition do we intend to work with them again. Adams told us one thing, told the Governor another thing, and told the people something else; and we're not trusting to work with him again. If you want to try, you will find out what we're telling you is true.' They offered me a coalition under my leadership. Brancker and I discussed the matter, and I said to Brancker, 'We can't do it. We've been fighting these people too hard. We've fought them tooth and nail for many years and it is impossible to think about working together with them on the Executive Committee.' But the mistake I made was not to realize that the country had returned them too. Anyhow, I declined the offer.

About two days afterwards, I was in my office, and a man called Ulric Grant (the same chap that was involved with the disturbances and got ten years) walked in and said that Grantley was asking me if I would give him a coalition. I said, 'He must have heard that we refused the one with Wilkinson and Walcott. We can discuss it. We can meet in the Assembly chamber and discuss it. My Executive will come and he can bring his.' So Adams said he would come with Hugh Springer and that he would not bring anybody else. But I had Brancker, Lewis and the entire Executive of the Congress Party in the wing of the House of Assembly. Adams was very late in coming, so we rang Hugh Springer to find out why he had not come, but Hugh said he did not know anything about the meeting at all. Then Grantley came in late and said he was sorry he was late. He was in a hurry but he could speak for himself and Hugh Springer. Eventually, we told him we would tie the coalition up with him, provided our two seats on the Executive Committee were filled by Brancker and myself, and that he could nominate the other one for his Party. There were four seats.

He left us to go to Government House to advise the Governor, Sir Hilary Blood. That was probably on the Thursday because the Friday evening I was in the office working when he rang me to tell me that the Governor had refused to take Brancker. I told him that the Governor could not refuse to take Brancker. He said, 'Well, you see, when Brancker was a student in London, he got mixed up with Sir Oswald Moseley's Fascist Party'. I said, 'What does that have to do with it?' Brancker was a young chap then and a lot of Barbadian scholars since then have been mixed up with the Communist Party. He said that, as the Governor had actually refused to accept Brancker on the Executive Committee, he had therefore nominated Hugh Blackman. My reply was, 'You have no right to nominate anybody from my party.' I immediately telephoned Brancker and said that we would have to call off the agreement.

We knew that Brancker had joined Moseley's party at one time but we could not see what it had to do with a seat on the Executive Committee then. I tried to struggle along with the coalition but we differed in many ways with the policy which Adams was following. When I saw what was going on, I knew that the coalition could not last. I went to the Governor one day and, for the first time, he told me that Adams had never mentioned Brancker's name at all. He told me that Adams had reported to him that we had decided to put Blackman and myself on the Executive Committee. Both Brancker and myself had made the error of thinking that what Adams had said was true. We never thought it was possible for a man to lie so brazenly. I told the Governor it was not true and that, at the end of that session, if Brancker was not nominated for the Executive Committee, we would break up the coalition.[5]

We had a meeting of our Executive and decided that we had to break up the coalition if the matter was not settled satisfactorily. The Governor called in Adams and confronted him with the truth. Adams immediately went to Brancker and told him that I intended to break up the coalition, and, if I resigned from the Executive Committee, he would offer him my place. Brancker said, 'You told us that the Governor said that they could not have me because I was a Fascist and now you come to offer me a seat with you?' Adams said, 'Me? I never said that. What I said was that Blood told me that the Government House dossier had something against me, Adams, not you.' Brancker said, I don't even want to talk to you, man.'

Adams tackled Blackman next. 'You know, Blackman, I nominated you from the beginning. You owe something to me.' He then went to other members of the party who refused to accept the offer of a seat on the Executive Committee. Brancker refused, Wilson refused, but Talma accepted. The Party Executive had a meeting at Garner's house in St Philip and each member signed an agreement that we would not enter the coalition again unless the Party's two nominees, Brancker and myself, were on the Executive Committee. As a matter of fact, Talma himself drafted it. The first time we knew that Talma had agreed to accept Adams's offer was the following Sunday when I received a telephone call from Dan Blackett who told me, 'Man, I got a shock for you. I was at a meeting in St George just now, and who do you think was on the platform with Adams?' I said, 'Who?' He said, 'Talma. He told the people he was with Adams again because he was in the party with Adams before us.' This broke up the coalition. In the ensuing 1948 election, the Congress Party had several meetings in Christ Church explaining what Talma had done, and he lost his seat. He came back in the election after that, however.

This is my considered opinion now: the biggest error of my entire political life was refusing to accept the offer made by Wilkinson and Walcott of a coalition with the Conservatives under my leadership. The Conservatives knew that it would be impossible to work with Adams again. The Congress Party had a programme at that time which was such that they would have had to agree beforehand with some of the main items; otherwise we would not have agreed to join them. I am absolutely sure now that if I had gone to the country with the programme we had agreed upon, taken from our manifesto, we could have achieved a great deal.

Adams had a certain amount of interest in constitutional reform, and so did I. As a matter of fact, we had both tabled resolutions calling for adult suffrage on the same day. There were, however, many other things besides constitutional reforms that in themselves were important. There was the question of improving the island's economy and fostering the tourist trade. One example of this is that Pan American Airways applied very early for permission to come in here, and it took us a few years fighting in the House of Assembly to get the government under Adams to agree to the entry of that airline. One of the rows which E.K. Walcott, as Attorney General, and the Governor had, was over that, because it meant opening up the island to American tourists, and the British did not want it. The British at that time owned British West Indian Airways before Trinidad took it over. What became BWIA was started as a small enterprise by a man called Yerex from New Zealand. Adams actually said on the floor of the House that the British had said that, if Pan American came here, BWIA would be squeezed like a concertina.

There is a story attached to how I finally succeeded in getting Pan American to come here. I went to America shortly after the war against Japan ended and the Americans were transporting troops across the country as they came back from the Pacific. It was impossible to get a plane passage or even a train ticket from New York to come down to Barbados. I tried for months to get a train to take me down to Florida where I thought I might be able to get a plane to get out. I had booked three months ahead on a train and, fortunately, I did not go because it crashed somewhere in Alabama. I was told that the only way I might get out was to go down to Florida and try to get a flight from Florida to Trinidad. I had to take a Greyhound bus from New York to Florida. I left New York on a Saturday morning and I did not arrive in Florida until about 7.00 o'clock the Monday evening, changing buses all the time.

I nearly got killed in South Carolina. I was tired and had got wet and had the 'flu' and I had a lot of baggage. We stopped in South Carolina at a restaurant and washroom where the passengers were going in to shave and get something to eat. So I started to follow them. I knew about the racial prejudice in the South, but I really was not aware of its extent. So I followed the white passengers to the restaurant and left my bags just outside the door. A chap inside the restaurant came flying out and grabbed me by the waist and pushed me outside. So I put my other bag down to knock him down and he held my two hands and said, 'Man, you want to get killed? If you make another step in there, that man has a gun to put a shot in you. You cannot come in here. You ought to know that.' So I said, 'What nonsense are you talking! All passengers on the bus have gone in there to eat and I was going to eat too and probably get a shave.' He said, 'You negroes can't come in here. You have to go outside and come around the side, beside the kitchen. There we have a little hole in the kitchen and we give you a sandwich and a cup of coffee if you want it. But you cannot come into this restaurant.' He took me around the side of the place and gave me a cup of coffee and a sandwich. So I stood up there and ate it. It was terrible in those days down in the South.

I got back on the bus eventually, changed to another bus, and went on down through Alabama and Georgia, right into the deep South. We had to sit in the two back seats. At certain stops the agricultural labourers would get in with their hoes and forks and knives in the two back seats with me.

Eventually I got down to Florida on the Monday evening. The next morning I went down to the Pan American Airways office to try to see if I could get out. All the clerks said, 'Mr. Crawford, it is impossible. You could stay here for months.' I decided that I had to get home because otherwise I would have lost my seat in the House. I had only about a week or two more before it would have been declared vacant and there would have had to be a by-election. Eventually, I did not tell them why, but I told one of the ladies there, 'It is absolutely imperative. I must get back within a week at least.' She promised that she would see what she could do for me. Of course, they were all white. She said, 'You keep in touch with me and I will see what I can do.' So I rang her in a couple of days and she said, 'Nothing doing yet.' Then one morning she rang me very excitedly, 'Mr Crawford, come down. Come down right away. I have two American lieutenants going to Puerto Rico. I will take one off the flight and put you on it, and from Puerto Rico you should be able to get to Trinidad quite easily.' So I went flying down and she gave me this ticket to go to Puerto Rico. I was so grateful, I said to her, 'You have been very kind. I don't know how I am going to repay you for your kindness but, at least, if you would like it, you can have dinner with me at my hotel before I leave tomorrow. She said, 'Sure! Yes Sir.' I said, 'When I go home I will tell my landlady.' I was on private business then.

I went to my hotel from the Pan American office that morning and told the landlady that one of the ladies from Pan Am had been kind enough to get me a seat on the plane and the least I could do would be to have her to dinner in the hotel the evening before I left. She nearly had a stroke. 'What? This negro came all the way from the West Indies to get the Yankees to blow up my hotel tonight?' She said, 'Do you think you can bring a white lady in here to dinner? They would put a bomb in the hotel tomorrow morning. You don't believe there are Yankees around here?' I said, 'All right. All right. Not to worry your head.' I telephoned the lady and I said, 'I am very sorry. My landlady objects.' So she said, 'Mr Crawford, I understand'. I said, 'Well, thanks very much indeed, but if you ever come to the West Indies, I owe you a dinner.' And that was that. This racism plague was really rampant then.

Years after that I went to Miami with Frank Odle, my Permanent Secretary at the time, and that same landlady had us to lunch. She wrote me a letter once saying she was going to Havana for a vacation and she wanted to know whether I was going to be in Barbados. She would take a bus to come to see me!

Well, I left the hotel to go to the airport with this ticket. When I got there, the plane was about four hours late so I went to the restaurant to get something to eat, and the man in charge told me not to come in because he could not serve me in there. I said, 'I am a passenger like all the other passengers going by that plane and they are eating in here and I don't see why I can't eat.' I was getting near home now, so I was not prepared to put up with any more insults. He said, 'You cannot be fed in this restaurant. We don't feed negroes in here.' I said, 'Where is the manager?' He said, 'He has gone home.' I said, 'Get him on the phone. I want to talk with him.' He said, 'He has gone home.' I said, 'Get him at his home, I want to talk to him.' So he rang the manager. I said, 'I am here at the airport with a ticket to go to Puerto Rico on your plane and my name is W.A Crawford and I am from Barbados. The man at the airport told me I cannot get anything to eat here at all. I've got to go outside somewhere to get it. Well, I cannot leave the airport. I am going to tell you something: you had better come down here right away and see that I get something to eat. If not, I am going to telephone Mr Juan Trippe (he was managing director of Pan American Airlines and as such he knew of the battle I and other opposition members of the House were waging to get Grantley Adams's government to pass legislation to allow Pan American to come to Barbados) in Washington immediately and tell them that Pan American will never get to Barbados.' I had been fighting here like the devil to get Pan American to come in here at the time, with Adams opposing it, and here was this man telling me I could not eat at the restaurant. He said, 'Mr Crawford, don't telephone. I am coming down right away.' So he came soon enough from his house and he took me upstairs to the VIP lounge and sent me up a bottle of wine and some dinner. So I stayed up there in the VIP lounge by myself, where the congressmen, Presidents and so on stayed when they were passing through, looking down on the white passengers. When the plane came in, I came downstairs and got aboard. I only mention that to show how the fight we had to put up to get Pan American to come here at that time served a purpose.

When Brancker refused the seat on the Executive Committee which Adams offered, Talma took it. Lewis defected and so did Blackman. After the 1948 elections Adams offered to make Garner Minister of Agriculture if he would leave the Congress Party, and he accepted it. I had put him in the parish but in any case the people had not been satisfied with him.

James Christopher Mottley was another member that I had shepherded along. Another parishioner called Catlyn had told me about him. He was at that time a local preacher in the Methodist church at Rices and was a fairly good speaker because he practised in the church and that gave him a certain fluency. He spoke for the first time at a meeting I held in Queen's Park to drum up support for getting a quota for Barbadian agricultural workers to go to work in America. After that, he spoke during my campaign, so when Garner defected and went to Adams, I offered to run him in St Philip. The people did not like him at first, possibly because they thought he was not of the right calibre to be in parliament, but I thought he would be useful.

When he got into the House in 1951, I went to the Bank of Nova Scotia and backed a loan which I told him he could pay back from the little salary he got from being a member. He bought some suits. I advised him to borrow some more money and put houses on some land he had at Rices so that he could rent them out and be assured of an income when he got too old to work. To my surprise, one day he voted in the House with Adams against me. When I asked him about it, he told me that Adams had promised him that he would make his daughter and son-in-law head teachers if he would leave me and vote with him. As head teachers, they would get good pensions and be able to support him. I had picked the man up from nothing and he had me really fed up. Adams reneged on his promises later, and the headships were not forthcoming. Mottley wanted me to intervene on their behalf with Rawle Jordan, the Chief Education Officer, but I refused. He could not run in the parish again because the people of St. Philip would not have voted for him after the way he had treated me. Afterwards, it seemed that his financial status declined, so I always showed him some kindness when I went his way.

Adams used them all. He used Garner; he made Talma lose his seat in Christ Church after he defected from the Congress Party. These defections can be explained mainly by the fact that most of the people in politics at that time had no independent means and that left them open to the type of influence that Adams could exert. That was one of the reasons why Adams lasted. In the House, too, they had to follow him like sheep whether he was right or wrong because they depended for their livelihood on the little money they got in there. Adams used to budget for a surplus and this surplus was sent abroad to invest to build up countries that were far more developed than we were. When we started opposing this, for instance, the people in Adams's party still voted for him. They just could not do otherwise. Hugh Springer left politics very early; and I do not think that he and Adams got on very well.

It was not politically feasible to build up a party merely to give Adams more seats. In the circumstances of the time, the man who could control patronage could grab the others. Therefore the Congress Party was finally dissolved.[6]

Notes

1   There can be no verification of Kinch's allegation. However, Crawford, like Adams, tended to be damning about those whom he regarded as disloyal.

2   Atholl Edwin Seymour 'T.T' Lewis (1905–1959) was a rarity in Barbadian politics - a white man, a socialist, fully engaged in progressive politics. He represented the constituency of Bridgetown in the House of Assembly from 1942 until 1956, and was successively a member of Crawford's Congress Party, 1944–1947, the Barbados Labour Party, 1947–1955, and the Democratic Labour Party, 1955–1959.

3   The Liberal Association, founded in 1936 or 1937, was a relatively loose multi-racial association of individuals interested in the politics of moderate reform. It never attracted popular support and faded from the scene by 1940.

4   The actual breakdown of the parties' standing was: 9 for the Barbados Labour Party; 7 for the Congress Party; 7 for the Barbados Elector's Association (the Conservatives); and one Independent.

5   The governor's report on Nov. 25, 1946 to the Secretary of State for the Colonies seems to confirm that Adams did not nominate Brancker. He wrote: 'I asked him therefore to submit to me the names for the Executive Committee and he has put forward himself, Springer, Crawford and Blackman whom I have accepted.' However, there is no way of knowing whether this brief report represented the full exchange of views on the matter.

6   The Congress Party did fight the general elections of 1948 and 1951, winning three seats in 1948 and two seats in 1951. Presumably the party was dissolved in 1956, because Crawford was not a founding member of the Democratic Labour Party in April/May 1955, but he was one of its candidates in the 1956 general elections.

CHAPTER 10

Caribbean/American Links

*I*n 1938 I was invited to America by the West Indies Defence
Committee to give some first-hand information of conditions in
the West Indies, especially those which led to the disturbances in
the middle 1930s. As a matter of fact, I was in New York when the Jamaica
disturbances broke. They were the last in that period, April to June 1938.

The *Amsterdam News* was probably the second biggest black-owned
and published newspaper in the United States. It certainly was the biggest
black-owned newspaper published in New York City itself. It was owned
by two black doctors, one Dr Savoury from Guyana, and the other an
American, Dr Powell. Both medical practitioners were enjoying a very
lucrative practice and they bought this newspaper, which had a very good
advertising and editorial staff. They really made it a Negro paper to be
reckoned with in the States. The editor, who also was the Caribbean
correspondent for *Time* magazine, called me one day and said, 'I am supposed
to write something about these riots in Jamaica. I don't know anything
about it at all and, if you would be kind enough to write it for me for
publication in *Time*, I would reciprocate by introducing you to a friend of
mine called George Laton who is the editor of *Harper's Bazaar* and who I
am sure would be glad to get something from you on the West Indies.'

So I wrote the article for him on the general disturbances in the
West Indies with specific emphasis on the Jamaica uprising at the time,
and then I went downtown to the office of *Harper's Bazaar* where I
expected to meet the editor, George Laton.

Newspaper Headline

He was very glad to see me and he said, 'Mr. Crawford, you are just the man we want to handle something for *Harper's Bazaar*. What we want is an article from you drawing a parallel between what is going on in the West Indies now for the last four or five years and what we did in America to throw off the British yoke. In other words, we want a parallel between the West Indies now and the American war for independence from Great Britain.' I said to him, 'Mr. Laton, that is impossible. There is no comparison at all. Yours was a struggle for independence to throw off the British yoke, but the masses in the West Indies are not so much struggling now for independence as they are struggling for a better way of life. They want better educational facilities, better housing, better living conditions, better everything. It is not an anti-imperial struggle at all in my interpretation.' I outlined various aspects of the situation down here, and I told him that the masses were not armed. The only place in the entire West Indies in which any sort of mock military drills were being carried on was in Trinidad. The Oilfield Workers Union, led by their legal adviser, Adrian Cola Rienzi, used to perform weekly military drills on the San Fernando promenade, using broom sticks as rifles. That was an isolated case because Rienzi had been brought up with the Sinn Fein in Ireland, where he studied law. I really could not fulfil the promised assignment for *Harper's Bazaar*.

Incidentally, while I am at it, I had better refer to the circumstance that I also happened to be in New York sometime in the late 1940s when the Indonesian crisis broke and Sukarno, the Indonesian nationalist leader, threw off the yoke of the Dutch. A newspaper called *P.M.* was being published in New York at the time. It was an evening paper owned by a wealthy Chicago magnate, Marshall Field, and it was supposed to be the New York equivalent of *Paris Soir*, except that it carried no advertising at all. It was an attempt by Marshall Field to demonstrate that a paper could be published with strong progressive policies without advertising support. Naturally, it failed eventually. At the time there were two very distinguished journalists in New York, Werner and Lerner, one or both of whom contributed to the paper. I was asked to write a contribution to this paper on what I thought would be the likely effect of the Indonesian crisis on the Dutch colonies in the Caribbean, Aruba, Curaçao and Suriname. So I wrote the article and they gave it a middle-page spread with photographs of the Dutch West Indies and the Indonesian islands, with articles on both sides, one by Werner and one by me.

These articles created quite a stir. About two or three days after the paper appeared on the streets of New York, I got a call from a man called Paul Blanchard. Blanchard said, 'Mr Crawford, I am Paul Blanchard and I am an official of the State Department in Washington attached to the Caribbean section. Your article created quite a stir, and I have been deputed to get in touch with you to have a chat. I want to come down from Washington to New York and invite you to lunch at a restaurant of your choice.'

Blanchard came down a few days later and took me to lunch. We had a very long, interesting evening and I imagine that the authorities wanted to find out whether there were any nationalist firebrands in the area likely to cause trouble. He had written a book called *Democracy and Empire in the Caribbean* (1947) and he came down to the West Indies some time afterwards.

In 1938 I had travelled to New York by a ship belonging to the Canadian National Steamship Line which was owned by the Canadian government. These were three very comfortable ships which carried passengers and cargo from the West Indies as far as Halifax. There were some cargo ships, too, plying between Canada and the West Indies because Canada has always been one of the major suppliers of West Indian imports; and, I would like to say in passing that Canada has amply reciprocated by giving grants and gifts from time to time to all the West Indian countries. These three ships were subsidized by the individual West Indian islands according to what their treasuries could afford. Barbados, Dominica and St. Lucia all gave subsidies. The ships travelled

The Main Shopping Area, Broad Street in the 1950s.

Sugar Cane Cultivation in Barbados

Trafalgar Square, Bridgetown in the 1960s, now renamed National Heroes Square.

Tudor Street, Barbados in the early 1900s

Bridgetown Harbour in the early 1900s

The Ceremonial Opening of the New Deep Water Harbour

Aerial View of Deep Water Harbour

Trade Fair (Caribbean Exhibition), March 3, 1962.

Barbados' Minister of Labour, Mr. Wynter Crawford (centre), at a press and radio conference at government headquarters with Miss Phyl Clancey of Lyons Teashops and Mr. Pedro Welch, acting Labour Commissioner.

The Cabinet at a press conference.

Minister of Trade and Labour, Mr. Wynter Crawford (At head of table) conducts a press conference at government headquarters on the scheme to send hotel workers to Britain. Others from left are: Mr. Pedro Welch, Mr. N.L.W. Barratt and Miss Valerie Taylor. Backing are members of the press and radio.

Wynter Crawford

Wynter Crawford: Builder of Barbados

Torrey Pilgrim

Some contributions

"Wynter Crawford: Builder of Barbados," *Sun Nation*, July 31, 1988.

Statesman who earned his sleep

by Harold Hoyte,
Editor-in-chief

LOOKING BACK on it, I had to learn alot from Wynter Crawford.

As a youngster I discovered that our families were very close. As a schoolboy I was fond of researching newspapers and his Observer was the most reliable authority of the period of major social change in Barbados.

As a Harrisonian, I spent my Tuesday evenings after school in the House of Assembly, listening to the great ones of that era: M.E. Cox, Frank Walcott, Lloyd Smith, Cameron Tudor, Ronald Mapp, E.D. Mottley, Owen T. Allder, Wynter Crawford, among many stalwarts.

As one of the figures behind the launching of this newspaper, I relied heavily on Crawford's counsel which endeared right up to the end.

I am sure that over the past three weeks when I wanted him in hospital and he tried vainly to express himself and as he squeezed my fingers to recognise my presence, he was reinforcing all that he had shared with me in recent years.

The irony of our relationship is that I don't know how if I would have appreciated him as much had he gone on to capture the top political prize which seemed his to claim at the end of his career.

What I do know is that he has left an impressive record and an indelible mark on our country as a crusading journalist, a highly competitive politician and an ally of progressive forces for five decades.

On Thursday night he joined fellow Barbadians Sir Grantley Adams, Errol Barrow and Tom Adams in the great beyond after a distinguished and colourful career in public life.

But there was one more important difference

WYNTER CRAWFORD — AN APPRECIATION

between Crawford and the others. They knew what it was like to reach the mountain top. Wynter Crawford only got close to it.

Yet he can boast of having had a considerable hand in shaping the social revolutions which created the new Barbados.

He is one of only a few men who can claim to have been party to the launching of the political careers of the two great leaders of this country, Sir Grantley Adams and Errol Barrow. What is even more impressive is that his service endured the entire period.

His vision inspired important developments in immigration and industrialisation, the farm labour programme and a teenage-related wage scheme for sugar workers.

Also, it was from the prolific Wynter Crawford that first came concepts of a flour mill, a tannery, the east coast road, agricultural extension services but meals for school children and the establishment of the Hilton Hotel.

Few people know that it was the progressive thinking of the Congress Party that was the fulcrum for the Democratic Labour Party's popular programme of change in the 60's.

A founding member of the Barbados Labour Party and a member of the first BLP Cabinet, Crawford's real contribution to the advancement of Barbados cannot be limited to a part of the achievements chronicled under the leadership of either Sir Grantley or Errol Barrow.

His was the unique Wynter Crawford-crafted vision, many of them 20 years ahead of their time just as important, his vision was never circumscribed by the limitations of either of the two great parties of Barbados or indeed of his own less-heralded National Congress Party.

The powerful political figure that became Deputy Premier Wynter Crawford was shaped in the turbulent 30s when the country was crying out for strong black leadership and men of courage were scarce.

It was sharpened in the 60s when the country sought change and few wanted to wager their political future on a political platform that would oppose the then dominant BLP- but it was blunted in an ugly war against the giant Errol Barrow at his formidable best.

For a quarter of a century Crawford represented the people of St. Philip with massive majorities and seemed impregnable until he broke with the BLP. It was in the 1961 election that he lost in a memorable campaign which called for "no more winter in St. Philip."

It was a defeat that would hurt him deeply.

But his deeper political hurt was over what he called the lost opportunity for Barbados to give leadership "to these islands", a chance he thought we forfeited in 1966.

At every opportunity in recent years he has reminded me of where the region would have been if Barrow had grabbed that chance.

He also shared with me the pain he has carried all his life because neither BLP nor DLP governments would give due recognition to these who were associated with the disturbances of 1937 and the fact that the landmark date of July 26 is not a national holiday.

Here was a man who was in the vanguard of change for a new order with adult suffrage, equality, here was a man who charted a course for a modernised Barbados 20 years later and who tried but failed to encourage the formation of an independent East Caribbean federation as well, all with the fervour of a man possessed.

Crawford's falling out of grace, first with Grantley Adams with whom he never really got along, and then with Errol Barrow at the time of independence, cost him dearly in narrow political terms.

Indeed, only the courage of Prime Minister Tom Adams ensured that Crawford got some national recognition in 1982 when he was awarded the Companion of Honour. Without that achievement, the last 25 years of his life would have been tragically barren.

But those 25 years were not wasted. In one sense, thankfully, he has done more than both Sir Grantley and Barrow. His foresight ensures that we who are left behind and who will follow will benefit from reading his views as an important part of our history.

As a truly great batsman, Wynter Crawford wanted an innings that was not just full of fine strokes, impeccable timing, careful placing and good luck. He also wanted a very long innings.

In fact, he wanted two more things in life: an innings of 100 years and an opportunity to publish his memoirs.

He got a brilliant and defiant innings of 83 that ranks as a good 100 in my books. The task of publishing his memoirs will pass to others. What is important is that he completed the job of writing them.

With the death of Wynter Crawford Barbados has lost a real political stalwart, a trail-blazing journalist, a true patriot and a life-long fighter for the advancement of the masses.

He deserves to rest in peace

"Statesman who earned his sleep," Article from the *Sunday Sun*, December 5, 1993 every two weeks. I think that two of them were sunk by submarines during World War II. They were called, 'Lady Hawkins', 'Lady Drake', and 'Lady Nelson'. Incidentally, a friend of mine, Gladys Carmichael, was on the 'Lady Nelson' when it was torpedoed by a German submarine in the harbour at Castries. She had gone to St Lucia to see her father, Dr Timothy Howell, a dentist there for many years. The passengers had just boarded the ship which was scheduled to leave at 6 p.m., and she was in the cabin when this torpedo rocked the ship. Fortunately, Castries already had a deep water harbour, unlike the Bridgetown harbour at the time, and because the ship was attacked alongside the wharf, the passengers who were not injured scrambled to the deck and walked on to the street.

These ships generally travelled at night so as to spend the entire day at the next port unloading cargo and taking passengers. This gave the passengers time to go ashore and look around and see the places. The ships had three classes: first class, which was fairly elegant, second class, which was quite good, and the third class, which was fairly basic but had cabins. They also carried deck passengers between islands on the overnight run. Chairs were provided so that you could lie down and sleep. There was canvas over the deck and a lot of the hawkers from the islands used the decks. At one time, the way the ships ran, you could leave Barbados by one ship on the Friday night and get to St. Lucia the next morning early. If the Monday was a bank holiday, you could leave the Monday night and get back to Barbados in time for work on the Tuesday morning. A lot of Barbadians used to do this.

These ships went north from Guyana to Trinidad, to Grenada, to St Vincent, to Barbados, to St Lucia, to Dominica; then Montserrat to Antigua to St Kitts; then to Bermuda, which took two days, and from Bermuda another four days or so to Boston. The Lady ships were not supposed to take third-class passengers beyond St Kitts during the winter, or anytime for that matter, because the cabins were not heated. Between St Kitts and Bermuda it was fairly cool but on the way to Boston it became too cold for deck passengers.

I was travelling on one of these ships, the 'Lady Hawkins', on my way to Boston. At the time I had an aunt there, so I thought I would spend a couple days with her. Her first husband had died and she had re-married to Stafford Douglas, a cousin, who was the father of the former Chief Justice, Sir Randolph Douglas.

I was travelling second class and, after we left St Kitts (I think it was fairly early in the year around March) and were on the way to Bermuda, the steward in charge of second class came to see me early one morning.

He was a man called Phillips, the father of Erskine Ward's wife, Lady Ward. 'Mr Crawford' he said, 'I want to see you. We have some trouble here aboard. The passengers have complained to me, and I told them that I would discuss it with you. You are the only person I will discuss it with on board the ship. We have third class passengers going to Boston.' I said, 'What? It is impossible, man, because under the agreement between the West Indian governments and the Canadian government the ships are not supposed to take passengers between the West Indies and America other than in first and second class because there is no heating in third class cabins.' He said that was the trouble because they had passengers on the third-class deck, and they were all very scared because the night before they had nearly frozen to death, and they were so cold that they figured that, if they had to spend another night like that, they would die. He was not the third class steward but he knew me and came to me for help.

After breakfast, I went down to the cabins and talked to the people who were scared stiff. Later I went to the office of the ship and asked the chief steward to see the captain of the ship. 'The captain of the ship, what for?' he asked. I said, 'I would like to see him to have a chat with him.' I was in my twenties then. He said, 'I don't see what you would want to see the captain for.' I said, 'Well, I want to discuss with him something about the ship and, if I can't see him here, I will have to go up to his cabin. He said, 'O.K. I will phone and call him down.' So he phoned the captain. He came down and wanted to know what I wanted. I said, 'Captain, under the Agreement which we have with the Canadian Government to run the steamers, I think you know that you are not supposed to carry West Indian passengers lower than second class between St Kitts and Boston.' He said, 'What's your name?' I said, 'My name is Crawford. I am Wynter Crawford.' He said, 'What business is that of yours, Mr Crawford? I run this ship, not you,' and he was very haughty. So I said, 'Look, Captain! There are some third class passengers aboard this ship and they cannot remain there because, if they die, you will be responsible, as well as the agents in Barbados and the Canadian government.' So he said, 'Who runs this ship? How is this your business? I don't see how that concerns you.' I figured that I was on solid ground and was determined that he had to remove those passengers, so I said, 'I am the editor of a newspaper from Barbados. If you don't take those people from that third class cabin and put them in second where there is ample room for them, when I get back to Barbados you and the entire crew on this ship – everybody responsible – will be in a lot of trouble if anything happens to them.' At this point he called the purser out of the office and the two of them talked while they walked off and left me. I did not say anything more and walked off myself. About an hour later, Phillips, the second class steward, came to me and said, 'They are moving them out.' They were moving the passengers out from the third class into second. That's all I wanted. But, if I walked on deck after that and I saw the captain, I would walk somewhere else. I did not feel very safe at all with him on board the ship.

I was in the States for a few months and I swore I would not take that ship on the way back. In those days you could not fly to New York; you had to go by ship. There were several ships going to New York. There was the Furness Whitney Lines with two ships, one called *SS Dominica* and the other *SS Nerissa*. Then there were lines which plied between New York, Barbados, Rio, Brazil then back from Rio to Barbados to New York. Every two weeks, the *Volvan*, the *Vestris* and the *Vandyck* came here. The *Vestris* was sunk at sea and a lot of West Indians and American tourists lost their lives. The hero was a man called Lionel Licorish, a Barbadian seaman on the ship. He was in the sea swimming around and picking up every passenger he could find, putting them on life boats. Those ships used to bring a lot of Brazilian tourists to Barbados. My grandfather had a small guest house and I used to see a lot of Brazilians when I was a young boy.

It was my misfortune, on the way back down, to have to take the same ship I had hoped to avoid. The ships ran every fortnight but I could not get a ticket on the one before and I could not stay any longer. As soon as I got aboard the ship, I found myself facing the same captain but I managed to avoid him until we got to Dominica. I had lived in Dominica for six months about four or five years before, so, the morning the ship got there, I decided to go ashore and check up on my old friends. There was a lady on board from Guyana whom I knew, so I invited her to go ashore with me. We spent the day visiting friends and in the afternoon we went to the Roseau Club to have a few drinks. Unknown to us, the ship's schedule had been changed to leave at 5 p.m. instead of the usual 6 p.m. because it took on little cargo. We were in the club when I heard the siren blowing, so we got into a car and drove quickly down to the harbour. The ship was not alongside but was anchored outside. We got a small boat while the ship was blasting and blowing. Apparently we were the only people ashore; the captain saw us coming and was up and down the deck fuming. When we got near to the ship, he ordered the quarter-master to pull up the gangway and he said, 'Mr Crawford, you are delaying my ship.' I said, 'Well, normally you leave at 6.00 p.m.' Anyhow, it was time for the gangway to be up, so they pulled it up and he said, 'If you can get up on a rope ladder, you can get aboard.' So he made them throw a rope ladder to the other side of the ship. I wanted to get home because my things were on board the ship so I said to Fanny, my companion, 'You think you can make it?' She said, 'Well, I will try.' So I said, 'I will stay in the boat bottom in case you fall down.' So she climbed up this rope ladder and got aboard, and then I got on and climbed up with the small boat bobbing below.

I had to go to America by ship again after the war. There were no planes because any planes they had in those days were used to transport troops since the war in Japan had just ended in 1945. I left here aboard the *George Washington* en route to Florida. Over seven hundred students from Guyana and all the West Indian islands were among the passengers. This was the first time since the end of war that they were able to go to American universities. Some were going to Washington to Howard, to Tennessee, to Boston and New York, all over the States. A storm was blowing up in Florida and the ship was becalmed off Haiti for about two days. On the second night, the coloured people on board staged a concert in the salon and invited the captain and all the tourists. It was a very good concert. There were some very good coloured artistes on board; there was a girl Harriette – the sister of Derek Sealy, the cricketer. There was also a Trinidadian prima donna – Pierre de la Rosa – whose father was the late Sir Henry Pierre. (He was knighted by the British government and was honoured by the American government for outstanding medical services to Americans in Trinidad during the World War II.) Pierre de la Rosa had been trained at the famous Julliard college of music in New York and was a fantastic singer. There was an Indian girl, Micius, a pianist going up to Julliard, and quite a few actors on board. We had a Eurasian woman whom I knew, whose husband was an engineering hydraulic advisor to Roddam Development Welfare and was stationed in Barbados for a long time. Micius played and the Eurasian woman sang the Cole Porter songs, 'Night and Day' and 'Begin the Beguine'. But Miss Pierre was the star of the evening.

A lot of Indians were on board from Trinidad and Guyana. Most of them were going from Florida up through the States and they were taking all sorts of things up there. Eventually, the storm abated and we got to Florida. The officials began searching everybody passing through customs. So some Indian fellows took table napkins and wrapped them around their heads and when they went down to open up their valises they put a piece of white cloth there with something wrapped in it and told the customs officers not to touch that, because there was something special on it. After that, every Indian wrapped a napkin around his head, went down and put some white thing on top his belongings and none of the customs officials opened or searched their luggage.

I had a few things to straighten up in Florida since there was confusion between the Jamaicans and the Barbadians who were up there as immigrants reaping crops and cutting canes. They would fight in the camps and a few of my constituents from St Philip, whom I had helped to go there, had written me saying that somebody should try and do something before there was a disturbance among the West Indians, since the Jamaicans were belligerent wherever they were. I had promised that I would go as soon as I could. It was a private visit, nothing to do with the government at all. I went to a few of the camps in Florida and got the meals, the service and the living conditions improved for the Bajan men because I had a lot of St Philip people up there. We made certain arrangements under which some of their money had to be sent back to the bank for them when they came home. I remember a teacher, Mr Browne, who was from Blades Hill, St Philip but then lived in Massiah Street, St John. He did a lot for those workers. They sent the money back to him. He banked it and then managed to get credit for them from Mannings to get lumber to build houses when they came back.

Incidentally, aboard this ship was an outstanding lawyer called Alexander Luvy, an Antiguan. He was a lawyer in Nashville, Tennessee, where he lived with his wife, a librarian at Fisk University. I had met him once in Barbados, so I went to see them and she took me to the Agricultural and Industrial Institute in Nashville where they were, for the first time in the western world, experimenting with artificial insemination of animals. The only place that had done it before was Russia.

Luvy became famous. He was driving in Nashville when his car collided with a police patrol car. When the authorities sued him, he brought a counter-suit contending that the car line was on the wrong side of the road, and he won the case. During the height of the revolution led by the Reverend Dr Martin Luther King, Luvy represented most of the blacks who were jailed and had to appear in court. One night, southern racists dynamited and completely demolished his home in which he and his wife were sleeping. Fortunately, neither of them was injured.

I did not stay long in Nashville with Luvy because I was going up to Chicago to my friend, Bindley Cyrus, a very distinguished lawyer, who eventually became the Barbadian Consul in Chicago. He was very active in West Indian affairs. After living in Chicago for many years, he retired and came back to Barbados living at 'Merryhill' where the Barbadian Union of Teachers now has its headquarters. The Union bought it from his widow who was an American woman. His first wife was the daughter of Booker T. Washington.

Cyrus was a staunch member of the Republican Party in New York and when the Republicans won under Eisenhower he was offered a judgeship. He refused it but instead accepted appointment as a member of the Anglo-American Caribbean Commission. He attended all the annual and bi-annual conferences in each of the American, English, French and Dutch West Indies territories. The bi-annual conferences alternated between the territories. I remember attending one of these conferences in Pointe-à-Pitre, Guadeloupe, somewhere between 1947 and 1948. It was near election time here and I was fairly sure that Adams and the others had me selected because they figured I would not get back in time for elections. I did not take the point seriously.

During the war the Americans had acquired a number of bases in the West Indies in exchange for fifty over-age destroyers which gave the British fleet added strength at a time when they were hard-pressed by the Germans. The bases were constructed in Antigua, Trinidad, and British Guiana and a committee was set up to have some of the Royal Commission's recommendations implemented. It was mostly a talk shop as nothing ever happened after these conferences. But this one I attended in Guadeloupe was an utter absurdity. To begin with, it should never have been held there because Martinique and Guadeloupe had caught hell during the war. They had been blockaded by the Americans who did not want Vichy to extend its influence in this area. But they tried to do the best they could, I suppose.

The privations which the French in Martinique and Guadeloupe had to undergo during the war were quite incredible. They were cut off from supplies; they could not build anything; and all their hardware and building materials were in short supply because the Americans rigidly maintained the blockade. As a matter of fact, it was said that the French had shipped whatever gold they had from France to Martinique for safekeeping so it would not fall into Hitler's hands.

The conference took place shortly after the war ended, and they were then trying to rebuild Martinique and Guadeloupe. A new hotel had been erected in Guadeloupe, and this was supposed to be the headquarters for the conference. It was not completely finished. Typical of the French – I forget how many hundred rooms the hotel had – but in the gents and ladies' toilets there was only one section each for men and women. It was quite a spectacle after the conference started to see people queuing up in lines stretching half a mile down the road to get into those two places.

We went by steamer from Antigua to Guadeloupe. On board were the conference Chairman, Albert Gomes, Sir Hubert Rance, Governor of Trinidad, and Lady Rance. I think only the conference rooms were ready and we were housed all over Guadeloupe in private houses. We were told that people had volunteered to come for us in their cars to get us to the conference the following morning at half-past nine. I was lodged in a new house with hardly any furniture and no running water, in the middle of a cane field. The delegates from Antigua, Grenada, St Vincent were all there in a small house not too far from mine. In the morning I had trouble getting a bath as there was no water and the residents spoke only patois. Eventually, they brought me a tub with some water and I had my bath in the middle of the cane field. We had some kind of breakfast and sat there waiting for the cars to come and pick us up to go to the conference but up to 12.00 o'clock nobody had come. Then, about half past one, we saw a Coca Cola truck coming down full of bottles and crates, and Sir Hubert and Lady Rance were in this truck, thumbing a ride into Pointe-à-Pitre. Some of us got on the side of the truck. The conference began that afternoon about 3.00 p.m.

The arrangements were a little better after that. We got down at 10.00 a.m. or 11.00 a.m., but what went on there was unbelievable. The conference was scheduled to last fifteen or sixteen days but, to my surprise, when I tried to leave the island, I was told that I could not get out for about two or three weeks. Fortunately, the Admiral of the French West Indian fleet came in with two or three ships. There was a cocktail party aboard one afternoon and he invited the conference participants. I had met the press aide before, so I told him to ask the Admiral whether there would be any connections between Guadeloupe and Antigua before the units of the fleet left, and he said, 'Yes, we have a torpedo ship going over to Antigua in two days to collect mail for the crew and I could ask the officers to take you over.' So one of the officers agreed to give me his cabin on the torpedo ship and I left the conference before it was finished to go to Antigua in order to get to Barbados in time for the elections.

I always think there is some similarity between the Anglo-American Caribbean Commission and the more recent Caribbean Basin Initiative. The Moyne Report on conditions in the West Indies could not be published when it was first presented because it was said that it would give too much propaganda material to the Germans. So when America got the bases in Trinidad, St Lucia and Antigua from the British, they set up this Commission hastily with the intention of trying to correct a lot of the bad conditions and poverty in the area. I do not think it ever did anything much.

The Commission did analyse situations across the Caribbean and it did some important studies, particularly under the direction of Eric Williams. There were so many of the Moyne Commission recommendations that were never implemented. I knew Eric Williams and I knew some of his studies. As a matter of fact, when he came to Barbados he rang me one day and said he wanted to discuss some pamphlets which the Commission had just produced in Trinidad in connection with agriculture. He had written two or three pamphlets on improving agriculture in the West Indies. This must have been in the early 1950s and he was still a member of the Commission. I remember discussing the idea with him, and I also once tabled a resolution in the House of Assembly calling on the Commission to take steps to try to ensure that bauxite mined in the Caribbean was refined into alumina before it was shipped to Canada and made into aluminium. You know, all the bauxite in British Guiana and, eventually, Suriname used to be shipped in the raw state for refining by the Alcan Corporation of America and Canada. My recollection is that, when eventually some attempts were made to implement this suggestion to convert the bauxite into alumina, Eric Williams had a plan to set up a plant in Trinidad, but this was never done.

The West Indies Defence Committee was very active in New York propagating the notion of self-government for the West Indies. Prior to the Montego Bay Conference in Jamaica in 1947, a large conference comprising all the Labour and Progressive leaders in the West Indies was held in Kingston, to review the question of West Indian self-government and present a united front to the British for self-government at the conference in Montego Bay.

The costs of the passage to Jamaica and accommodation were financed entirely by the West Indies Defence Committee in New York. I remember that at that conference we had one A.A. Austin from Antigua, Grantley Adams, Frank Walcott and myself from Barbados, Bradshaw from St Kitts, Marryshow from Grenada, two delegates from Guyana, one from St Vincent and Vere Bird senior, from Antigua. Those who were selected by the Government to represent the islands went to Montego Bay afterwards. At Montego Bay, there were Grantley Adams, H.A. Cuke, Keith Walcott, the Attorney General, and myself representing Barbados. During the conference, I came to the conclusion that enough attention was not being paid to the issue of West Indian self-government and independence.

Creech Jones, Secretary of State for the Colonies, was the Chairman of the conference. In my opening remarks, I said that the West Indies were entitled to independence, and that it was time for the colonial system to be abolished in this area. I also said that, if the British West Indian people had to remain as colonials, they would prefer to be under the American flag rather than the British. This created a furore. At that time there was hardly a West Indian family in Barbados, St Lucia, Grenada, Antigua or Trinidad that did not have relatives in America. They were to a large extent dependent on the remittances from those families almost every month. The relatives would send down food packages and old clothes. Large numbers of Barbadians went to the post office to receive gifts and packages and money orders from their relatives in America and used these to maintain themselves. The only people who went from Barbados to England in those days from among the people were probably students whose parents could afford to send them to school in England or Barbados Scholarship winners. We got nothing at all from England. In those days the price of sugar was as low as possible and America was more of a haven. At least this is how the West Indians felt.

Albert Gomes did not agree with what I said at all. He did not think that the Trinidad people would agree with me either. Adams disagreed with me too, of course, but I was very adamant because I meant what I said. I remember that, after the conference, I went back to Kingston and Robert Bradshaw from St Kitts came to me at my hotel and said, 'Man I regret very much not being at that conference. I would have supported you one hundred per cent.'

This West Indies Defence Committee in New York (they had small committees also in Boston and Chicago but most of the members were active in New York) certainly kept alive the question of self-government for the West Indies, and did everything they could to foster it. At some time in the later nineteenth century, most of the islands that had Representative Government had reverted to Crown Colony Government. It was felt by some people that, in some instances, the British Crown was more progressive than the planters and merchants.[1] A British Governor toed the line on British colonial policy but he could not initiate anything, not in Barbados at any rate. In Barbados, the old Executive Committee was the instrument for formulating government policies and, after the system was changed to a sort of ministerial government, the power passed on to the Ministers.

I must say something about Adrian Rienzi from Trinidad. He was half-Indian. His father was a white man called Hutson, a Trinidadian solicitor, and his mother was an Indian, I understand. But he changed his name to Rienzi after the famous Italian patriot. I am of the considered opinion that the West Indies would have got independence long before they did had Rienzi remained in the forefront of West Indian politics.

While he was studying in Ireland he became associated with Sinn Fein. He once told me that on weekends he would go to the country with his associates and, when he returned to his digs in Dublin on Monday mornings, the police would come and search his fingernails to see if they could discover from the dirt under the nails in what part of the country they were making ammunition over the weekend. He qualified in Law but the British refused to call him to the Bar because of his association with Sinn Fein. He applied for permission to go to India to join Nehru and Ghandi in the struggle for Indian independence but he was not allowed to go. The authorities would not give him a passport, so he returned to Trinidad. It was only after Ramsay McDonald led the first Labour government in Britain in 1928, that Cipriani, who was then powerful in Trinidad, and knew McDonald, was able to get him to have

Adrian Cola Rienzi

Rienzi's position reversed. Rienzi was then practising in San Fernando and was soon appointed Legal Advisor for the Butler Trade Union Movement.

I was in New York around this time (1938), and the organizers of a World Youth Congress sent me an invitation to represent the West Indies at a World Youth Conference at Vassar College at Poughkeepsie on the Hudson River, upstate New York. They told me they wanted to invite a Trinidadian and that they were sending for Captain Cipriani but I advised them that, in my opinion,

Cipriani was then a bit too advanced in age to represent anyone anywhere at a Youth Conference and that the man they should get was Rienzi. An invitation was sent to Rienzi who replied to the effect that it was very fortunate because he was leaving Trinidad shortly. The Oilfield Workers' Union in Trinidad was sending him up to an oilfield in Ploiesti, Rumania, and to Baku in Russia to investigate conditions and wages of oil workers in the Russian and Rumanian oilfields. On the basis of what he found, he would on his return to Trinidad help the oilfield workers' delegation to the Commission established by the British Government under Sir Arthur Pugh to investigate conditions in the Trinidad oilfields after the riots. So he said he would be happy to come to New York on his way to England. Well, he came to New York, and he and I went to Vassar and spent the entire time up there.

To get back to Rienzi, he left New York after the conference. He was first going to see his wife who was still in England, and then going on to Dublin. But just then the Munich crisis broke. When Chamberlain went to Berchtesgaden to talk to Hitler, Rienzi was actually on his way to attend a Congress of the Second International in Glasgow. Everybody thought there would be war. So he returned immediately to the West Indies. He came to Barbados thinking I was here but I had not yet returned. I think it was J.E.T. Brancker who had him called to the local bar, and he returned to Trinidad before I got back here.

In Trinidad, Rienzi headed the delegation of the Oilfield Workers' Union to the Sir Arthur Pugh Commission and presented the demands, but he did not have the chance of course to go to Baku or Ploiesti. After that, he ran for the Legislative Council representing San Fernando. He won a seat and he was a terrific advocate in the Trinidad Legislative Council for improving conditions for the working classes in Trinidad. He soon superseded Cipriani. The government recognized he was a force to be reckoned with because he organised the oilfield workers in the South. These workers used to wear a special black shirt uniform like Mussolini's black shirts, and he used to drill them every afternoon with military precision on the Harris Promenade in San Fernando. They used broom-sticks like guns, marching like soldiers. The British were a bit afraid of them.

The British Governor in Trinidad, Sir Bede Clifford, was very scared of Reinzi and he immediately had Rienzi put on almost every important government committee. Eventually, it came to the point where Rienzi was up and down from San Fernando to Port of Spain almost every day attending different conferences and committee meetings. So Clifford said to Reinzi (this is what Rienzi told me some time afterwards), 'You know what, Adrian? It is a very tiring job to be up and down from Port-of-Spain to San Fernando every day and back up next morning to attend early meetings. We've got several vacant rooms up at Government House; why don't you sleep there some nights? You can have a room there.' So apparently Rienzi agreed.

I had to go to Trinidad during that time, and Sir Bede Clifford invited me to tea at Government House one evening. The invitation came from Cedric Cunard who had offered his services as aide-de-camp (ADC) to the Trinidad Governor so as to release an Englishman for more active service during the war. (In the West Indian colonies, the ADCs were all English but, during the war, we had a Barbadian acting as ADC to the Governor, Sir Mark Young. He was Sir Laurie Pile's grandson, Lisle Sealy.) In the course of conversation, Sir Bede said to me, 'Oh, you know, your friend Adrian and I are very friendly. We actually go to the calypso tents at night and all that kind of stuff.' I was really very surprised, but by this time Rienzi used to sleep at Government House fairly often at night.

Later in the year, Rienzi went down to San Fernando one afternoon. The oilfield workers had a newspaper called *The Vanguard* edited by Ralph Mentor, one of the leaders of the union. Ralph said to Rienzi, 'You can't run next election. You would not get any support at all. People are not going to vote for you. The rumour has spread that you are very thick with the Governor and you cannot represent the people if you represent the Governor too. You would be wasting time to run again.' Reinzi told me he made some enquiries and found out he could not get any votes at all. He went to Sir Bede and said, 'I have landed myself in a kettle of fish in San Fernando with my voters: they think I am too thick with the Government.' I think he realized where the rumour had spread from. So he said, 'Once I can't run, I will have to take a Government job and I cannot go in as magistrate. I will have to be appointed to the higher echelons in the service – probably Crown Attorney or Attorney-General.'

Sir Bede said to him, 'Well, I am very sorry, Adrian. If I brought you in anywhere near the top, it would cause a lot of confusion in the Civil Service among the legal departments there. I will bring you in at a lower level. But I will make it perfectly clear in your dossier that the first time one of the higher posts becomes vacant it is to be yours.' So eventually Rienzi had to give up his seat in the Legislative Council. He did not run again and he took a job as a junior Crown Counsel with the understanding that as soon as a senior post became available he would get it.

Sir Bede Clifford left Trinidad on promotion and, sometime after that, one of the senior posts became vacant and Rienzi told the then Governor that he expected it according to what Clifford had told him; and that if he looked in his dossier he would find Clifford's recommendation for him to get the post. The Governor said, 'Rienzi, I am very sorry. I see absolutely nothing about that from Clifford in your dossier, and we can't appoint you.' So Rienzi was very disappointed and disheartened, and he had to remain in the same post for quite a while. At this time he again applied for permission to go to India but it was refused. I am not sure if he ever got promoted but I was surprised when he died. If he had remained in politics, it is possible that self-government would have come sooner. It is a question of not thinking about possible interpretations of behaviour; he was not bought out really.

I had a similar experience myself. When I was on the Executive Committee in Barbados in 1946–47, I presented a resolution one day for discussion. It was a proposal that the big offices in Bridgetown and the banks and big businesses should be compelled by legislation to employ a certain percentage of coloured people. In those days, it was impossible for any coloured person to get a job in a bank or big business office. Well, I got no support for it at all on the Executive. The Acting Governor was a man called John Rankine. He was really the Colonial Secretary but the Governor was away so he was Acting Governor. After the meeting, he said to me, 'Mr Crawford, I would like you to remain for a while. I want to have a chat with you.' So I remained (this was at Government House) and he said to me (I don't know how seriously), 'I am very sorry your resolution fell through for lack of support. Personally I did not agree with it myself, but I understand the point. What I think we should have in Barbados is small groups where coloured people and certain whites can meet occasionally in small numbers and then, eventually, we can extend the numbers so as to remove a lot of this racial prejudice. I understand that at your house at Pegwell you have a very efficient system of market gardening with irrigation.'

I had an overhead system of irrigation on my farm at Pegwell, and I grew vegetables. At one time Sam Marshall from Eckstein Village and myself sent a shipment of carrots and beets to Canning Ltd. in Trinidad and to Meat and Ice in British Guiana. It was an overhead irrigation system with a booster pump and overhead lines. People used to park their cars on the top of the hill near Christ Church parish church and watch this when it was operating. You would think the rain was falling. Rankine continued, 'I would like you to invite me to your house to see that system of irrigation. Any evening you like I would come up and see it.' So I said, 'I should be delighted to have you, Mr. Rankine, but I am leaving the island shortly and, as soon as I return, I would be happy to extend the invitation.' I never did invite him when I came back because I figured that the moment anybody heard that John Rankine had come to my house that would cause a serious political problem for me.

I do not think that there was any question of Rienzi selling out. I think he really was too preoccupied at the time to appreciate fully the wiles of a British governor. I think Clifford really tricked him, because Sir Henry Cunard was down there, and when Clifford said to him, 'Let's go to the tents' he went with him. Clifford was quite a playboy. He must have been like Major Peebles who had been an administrator in St Vincent and against whom I was to run later in St Philip.

I knew B.L. Barrow through my father, and I had heard that he was a man who had gone abroad for some time and had come back and opened a grocery and eventually acquired large acreages in the parish of St John. He ran for the House of Assembly and he was elected for one session, 1944–1946. When he was campaigning, the leader writer of the *Agricultural Reporter* wrote a very scathing and disparaging article suggesting that he should stay and mind the salt fish and salt pork. But I found Barrow a very interesting man to talk to. Anytime I was in the parish of St John and had a spare moment, I would go over to his house for a minute and chat. He still has two daughters living. He has a daughter still running the business, Mrs Bridgeman, and he has another daughter who was married to the late Eustace Gill.

Eventually, after several attempts, he got in the St John Vestry and later became churchwarden. One day I stopped in at his house for a chat and we were reminiscing about the old days when the planters completely controlled the political activities in the parish. Until he succeeded, I do not think there was a coloured man in the Vestry at all. Sir Laurie Pile, a big St George and St John sugar baron, was churchwarden at the time. At the first meeting of the Vestry, Sir Laurie Pile got up and formally welcomed Barrow. He said, 'Mr. Barrow, we are very pleased to have you in the Vestry with us, and we hope you will cooperate with us on issues affecting the parish. I want you first and foremost to remove those doubts in your mind that we don't want you here, because we have heard reports that you have said that the white people don't want you in the Vestry at all and have done everything to keep you out. We have never had any animosity or antagonism against you.'

Barrow told me that he listened very carefully and, when Sir Laurie sat down, he said, 'Sir Laurie, I want to thank you all very much for your welcome. First, let me assure you that I am more than willing to cooperate with you on anything in the interest of the parish. I want first and foremost to destroy this report that I said I do not like white people. That is not true because, you know if you go down to my house at Massiah Street now, and you look in my pig pen, you will see a white man cleaning it out.' He had one of those Poor Whites working in his pig pen. Barrow said to me that the next morning up to 10.00 a.m. he did not see the man come to work. So he asked one of the other employees what had

Francis Godson, Methodist Minister

become of him. The reply was, 'He is not coming back, sir. This morning early Mr Pile sent and offered him a job down at his place.' Barrow told me this himself and I was surprised sometime later to hear a young lady at the Barbados Museum say that somebody connected with the Museum had told her that story.

I would hope that at sometime the name Francis Godson will be remembered and cherished in Barbados as the first person in the island ever to talk about old age pensions. He was an Englishman who was the Methodist Minister at Bethel and he lived in Chelsea Road. He used to pester everybody in public life, including newspaper men and politicians, to help the old people. He would come into my office and say, 'Mr Crawford, I have a new list here this morning. I have added what the cost is to buy the basic necessities – the rice, the potatoes, the sugar, the milk – which would support an old person for a week, and it amounts to 48 cents. It would be so beneficial if the government would only devote some of the revenue every year to giving these people a little something.' He would leave me and go to different people from whom he thought he could get support for his scheme. He badgered everybody until eventually the Governor – I think it was Sir Mark Young – decided to recommend an Old-Age Pension with a Means Test for people over 65. The pension was 48 cents a week in 1940. Old age pensions now get about $40.00 per week.

Cheddi and Janet Jagan

This pension was due entirely to the persistence of the Reverend Francis Godson; and in return for what he had done, the Governor appointed him to serve for a while on the Legislative Council. No Bajan at that time showed such concern for indigent old people.[2]

I knew the Jagans for years. I first met Janet in Barbados while she was staying in the old St Lawrence Hotel. This must have been during the war when N. E. Wilson ran a small hotel in Fontabelle. I remember there was a dance there one night and Janet Jagan was here and I took her. Later in 1946, I went to Guyana where one of my sisters was married to a Guyanese and I went down there in 1946 and, between Janet and her husband whom I met there for the first time, and another girl who became Minister of Education under Burnham, a party was held for me one night at Jagan's house.

The Governor, Sir Gordon Gettesburg, invited me to tea one afternoon, but I went to Jagan's tea party first and Jagan said that he would take me to Government House. Janet said, 'You had better not take Wynter. You know you and Gordon don't get along at all. I will take him myself.' We used to keep in touch regularly after that. As a matter of fact, once Janet came in here and had trouble with the airport authorities. We were attending the opening of Parliament and all my party members, 'T.T.' Lewis, Brancker, Talma and myself, left parliament after the opening ceremony was finished and went straight to the airport to meet her. On another occasion, Cheddi came here and he was not allowed to land but he told the police he had come to see me and the police phoned me and asked if I would be responsible for him during his stay. I remember the last occasion I saw Janet which must have been in the 1960s. She came here to attend a meeting of the Family Planning Association and there was a big reception down at Sandy Lane for the participants. She asked me to take her down, and I did. They were having an election campaign in British Guiana then, and their party (PPP) was running as well as D'Aguiar's (UF) and Burnham's party (PNC). She said to me on the way down, 'We should be in big trouble if Burnham went and joined D'Aguiar and opposed us.' So I looked at her and smiled, and said, 'Come off it, Janet, you know very well that is what you would like to happen because if (she probably hoped I would suggest this to

Burnham whom I knew as well) Forbes Burnham was so silly as to go and join D'Aguiar, you would have it made. Then you would lambaste him as being the same conservative as D'Aguiar and you would win the elections hands down.' So she laughed because that was her intention. She clearly wanted me to associate Burnham with D'Aguiar.

Janet came back here on another occasion after that when she was extremely tired after a campaign. She said that she had travelled all over the interior campaigning, sleeping at night on the floor in huts. One night she had been sleeping on the floor somewhere in the forest and woke up to see a snake not too far from her. She used to work very hard. She and her husband have done a fantastic job of spreading communism in the Caribbean, starting from scratch. Once they sent some Indians who were holidaying here to see me. I invited them home one afternoon and I was absolutely struck as to how indoctrinated they were with this communist business. I think that history will record that the two of them almost single-handedly spread communism right through the British West Indies and the Caribbean, starting with small cadres in different islands. They probably sent them literature, and people paid visits. They were banned from some islands. They indoctrinated British Guiana.

All the communists in British Guiana have become communists through their influence, whether there were a few or many. I would not be surprised if their influence and activities spread to Suriname too. But I know that all the little communist cadres that existed in the other islands in the West Indies were almost all created by the Jagans. I do not mean the latter-day people like those in the universities, but I would say those before that.

Cheddi used to travel through the islands pretty often. I always got the impression that they had contacts in the area – in St Lucia and Dominica and Grenada. He never discussed them with me. For all the years I knew them, we never once discussed communism or Marxism or any politics. Communism was fostered also by a few scholars who went to London University and were put under the influence of Harold Laski, and he did a good job of indoctrinating them too.

Quite a few of Laski's students were under the influence of Gallagher. He was one of the two Communist members in the British House of Commons in the 1930s and 1940s. The other was called Zilliacus. One, I think, belonged to the Third International and the other to the Second. But both were Marxists. I know for a positive fact that Gallagher, too, had some influence on some of the West Indians studying in London. But, all in all, I think that Jagan did a thorough job spreading Marxism.

I am not talking about socialism because most of the progressive parties in the West Indies are supposed to be socialist but they are not communist.

A lot of Jagan's disciples would be pretty old now, but a lot of them would be young people too. Janet is very bitter against the U.S.A. because she is a Rosenberg. It is said that she was related to the Rosenbergs who were electrocuted for giving information about the atomic bomb to the Russians. He was supposed to have been a very close relative of hers and, from the time they were electrocuted, naturally she became very antagonistic towards the U.S.A.

Sometime around 1956 or 1957 I was very tired and thought I needed a rest. One morning I went down to Barclays Bank and borrowed some money and went to Haiti on a trip. Well, I had never gone to Haiti and I always thought I would like to go since it was one of the few places in the Caribbean that I did not know. Before I went there, I asked a friend, Albert Guiler, who I thought might have connections in Haiti, if he knew any persons there. 'Yes, you know that I import things like mauby bark from Haiti.' He used to operate the Bornn's Bay Rum factory and used to export a lot of Limolene and Bay Rum and other products to Haiti. He said, 'I have a friend there who is in the army – Lieutenant Hermanos. I will write him and tell him you are coming.'

Lieutenant Hermanos was kind enough to meet me at the airport. He had a business place in Port-au-Prince where he sold articles mainly for tourists. He also had quite a huge bond just outside the city. It could have been probably 5,000 – 6,000 square feet, in which there were all sorts of large containers and shelves. This bond was filled with barks of trees and herbs and bushes and there were individual shelves packed with barrels and boxes. He told me that this was a big operation connected with an estate. The estate had different trees from which medicine was made and his workers picked the bark and the leaves which were packed in boxes and shipped to London, New York and Germany to pharmaceutical companies to make medicine. He also showed me the bark from which quinine was made.

One morning while we were in the place, which was not too far from the university, there was a man coming down the street who was a friend of Hermanos; and there was another man coming down on the other side. Ton Ton Macoutes went to arrest this second man, and the first man shouted to them, 'Colonel, what you went and troubled that man for? He has not done anything.' So the Ton Ton Macoutes immediately left their victim alone and turned and arrested the man who had shouted. Hermanos said to me, 'That is the man they really intended to arrest. You will never see him again.' I also saw a few people in front of the university protesting against something, and two of the women were shot dead not far from where we were. Then in the afternoon I stayed in a hotel which was probably owned by the government. It was very near to the casino in Port-au-Prince. I was in parliament then, but I never thought of contacting any member of the legislature or any official. Probably it was a good thing because my passport said I was a journalist and, about a month before I went there, Duvalier had had an English journalist put in prison for nothing at all. Anyhow, in the afternoon, Hermanos came for me and he and his wife and sister took me to a place in the mountains where they spent the summer holidays. You go up this mountainside and on the way back down on the right side, there is a restaurant called "Le Persoir" perched on the mountainside with an entire front of glass. So when you go into "Le Persoir", you can see the entire city of Port-au-Prince lying at your feet. It is a beautiful sight. There were some beautiful hotels too. I spent a little over a week there. Before I left, Hermanos became ill and was put in the army hospital. I went to tell him good-bye at the hospital.

About a month or so after I returned to Barbados, I got a letter from him post-marked from New York, and I wondered what had happened. He said that, shortly after I left, at a party one night, Papa Doc Duvalier turned to some of the ladies and said, 'I have not seen Hermanos at one of my parties for quite a while. He has not come to one recently.' At two o'clock that morning, his phone rang and somebody told him what Duvalier had said. That was the signal which meant that between then and daylight the Ton Ton Macoutes would have come for him. He escaped from the house and hid and then eventually managed to get to New York. He could not go back to Haiti at all. Just as simple as that. The dictatorship of Duvalier was unmistakable.

When I left Haiti I went to Santo Domingo and, at the customs, I spoke to some officials and told them that I wanted to spend a couple of days to see the place and they said, 'You are welcome, sir. We have very nice hotels in Trujillo City.' But when I looked around the airport I saw armed soldiers with guns and bayonets. The entire airport was bristling. Everywhere I looked there was nothing but armed soldiers and policemen with guns and bayonets patrolling the place, so I got scared and got back on the plane. I never left the airport at all. It was too much for me; you could not feel safe. I stopped off in Puerto Rico for a few days and then came home.

Notes

1 This was certainly the view expressed by Crawford himself in the House of Assembly as early as June 1941: 'It would have been far better for us to have had Crown Colony Government rather than .... Representative Government, which is merely a farce of representation.'

2 The Rev. Francis Godson, an Englishman, came to Barbados in 1921 to serve as a Methodist minister. He distinguished himself as a social worker and social activist during the 1920s and 1930s, to the extent that he was popularly known as the Poor People's Friend and Father of Old Age Pensioners.

CHAPTER 11

Promoting Emigration And Land Settlement

By the time I got into the House of Assembly, I had the firm conviction that the island could go forward further and faster than it was heading. I began to pursue my own course in the House, with Adams opposing everything I introduced. Only Brancker supported me during the first session (1940–42). From time to time I raised the issue of some of the recommendations of the Moyne Commission, but to no avail.

I had long been thinking of the large-scale unemployment in the country and remembered that, as a boy, I knew two men, Bonnett and Nightingale, who used to come here every year to recruit people to go to Cuba to cut canes, and that a large number of Barbadians went each year. (Nightingale was the brother of Dr Nightingale who gave the St Michael's Vestry money for the Children's Home.)

This apparently had stopped. One day in 1943, I read that the Americans were selecting large numbers of people from the Bahamas to go to America to work in agriculture, picking fruit and different crops, and also to do some semi-skilled work to relieve Americans for the war effort. I thought it was an excellent opportunity to get some Barbadians outside again. I went to 'Chrissie' Brathwaite who had been a prominent member of both the House and the St Michael Vestry. I said, 'Chrissie, I want to hold a meeting in Queen's Park tomorrow night and I would like you to come and take the Chair.' He said, 'Can you get anybody else to go?' I said, 'There is a chap called James Christopher Mottley in St

Wynter Crawford leading delegation to Government House. From right to left: Crawford, McDonald Symonds, Dan Blackett

Philip whom I know. I might ask him to come down.' So we went to Queen's Park that night with 'Chrissie' Brathwaite in the Chair and Mottley as a speaker. Mottley spoke first and then I spoke, and I told the people that I had heard America was recruiting men from the Bahamas to go to work in Florida and Connecticut and different places like that, harvesting fruit and vegetables and cutting canes in Florida, and that I thought it was an excellent opportunity for us to try to get a quota to pick fruit too. I think it was the *Advocate* that reported that there were 10,000 at that meeting; I was told that it was the biggest crowd ever seen in Barbados. Anyhow, the meeting passed a resolution calling on the government immediately to send the Governor, Sir Grattan Bushe, and the Labour Commissioner, Mr Guy Perrin, to Washington to try to arrange with the authorities to get a quota for Barbados.

On Tuesday morning, Brathwaite and I carried the resolution to Government House to Governor Bushe, and on the same day I carried the same resolution into the House of Assembly. There were six members who were not planters. They had to support the resolution because the mob was with it, so the planters all voted for it. The big employers in those days liked the large surplus of unemployed labour because this permitted then to keep the wages down and keep the labour market depressed. They did not fancy the emigration at all. But they had to support it. It passed the House but there was one dissenting and critical voice, that of Grantley Adams. He was the only member who voiced any opposition, that he did not see any

use in passing a resolution because the Amer~~i~~
ships to carry munitions and cargo to the diff~~e~~
they going to get ships down here to carry Bajans ~~u~~
was passed without dissent.[1] So I took it to Govern~~
presented it to Sir Grattan Bushe. Within two days, Sir Gr~~a~~
Labour Commissioner went to Washington and within a week the~~
back saying that the U.S. government had agreed to accept Barba~~c~~
workers in the scheme. So Barbadian workers went up to America to pick
fruit and cut canes. It has been going on from then until now. As a matter
of fact, I myself went up there when there was some dispute between
Jamaicans and Barbadians, at my own expense in the 40s, to try to get it
straightened out, and I tried to get the programme extended.

I did the same thing in sending workers to Canada some years later
(in 1948). I had heard that in the Ontario basin and in the surrounding
areas the Canadian farmers could not get their fruit and vegetables picked.
I wrote two letters, one to the Minister of Agriculture in Ontario and a
similar letter to the Federal Minister in Ottawa, including excerpts from
recommendations made by appropriate US agencies showing the
contribution that Barbadians had made to the American war effort. I
suggested they employ Barbadian men. On the same day, I was going up
to the House of Assembly and Fred Goddard (MP for Christ Church) was
going in at the same time, so I said, 'Fred, look, I heard that they want
labourers in Canada in the Ontario basin, especially in the Niagara Valley.
They cannot get the harvests reaped and I have a resolution that I am
going to introduce. I want it passed today so I want it supported.' He said,
'I will second it.' That day I tabled it and we had it passed.

Within a short while, Barbadian workers were going up to Canada, and
the scheme is still in operation. I regarded it as a good contribution to the
economic situation in the country because it took off surplus workers and
sent them outside. They would remit their savings to Barbados, and when
they came back home, they had some money. There is no question that the
earnings from those workers almost changed the entire structure of Barbados,
in terms of housing for people and in the improvement of living conditions.
The government itself deducted a certain amount and sent it back to support
the families, and the balance was saved to give to them when they came
back. Within four or five years the entire structure and appearance of the
countryside were altered with the new houses going up from these savings.

Since then I have done a lot on my own – nothing at all to do with
the government – in trying to get people to go abroad. I went to Suriname
twice. There had been a small and unsuccessful emigration scheme to

name at one time and, when I went to Paramaribo and Marienbad the 1940s, I found three or four workers from Barbados still there. I tried to revive the scheme but the conditions in agriculture in Suriname were quite different. About two years after that, I went to Cayenne (French Guiana) to find out whether it was possible for some of our people to develop Cayenne because I had heard that some St Lucians were there. But I discovered that French Guiana was very undeveloped and there was nothing there at all. For all that, the place had tremendous potential being about the same size as Guyana.

As late as 1966, I went back to Cayenne because I had heard that the French government under De Gaulle had plans to establish a *base spatiale* – a space base – at a place called Kourou in the interior of Cayenne. I went up to Kourou, saw the place where they had planned to establish the base, and went back and spoke to the Prefect. I had taken down from the Labour Department a list of the wages we wanted for the different categories of labour and of the conditions like housing and all that kind of thing, and I presented it to the Prefect who told me that he would endeavour to do his best for us to get a quota to build the space base at Kourou. Nothing came of it because the Cayenne government contracted to get people from Nicaragua where wages were lower than what I had asked for the Barbadians. So they recruited all the people they wanted from Nicaragua. The base has since been built.

Even after I was out of politics, in 1972–73, my brother Lisle and I had to go to Brazil on business in connection with my paper-converting plant, and in Sao Paulo I discussed with the government officials the possibility of Bajans going to Brazil. We also talked about tourism at the time, but were told that, although there was a shortage of workers in Sao Paulo, which is the industrial heart of the country, there were more than enough labourers in the other places. Then we found that they were bringing in Japanese and that the Brazilian government had made a large area of land available to Japan. Farmers from Japan were cultivating the land and fishing and sending the harvests back to Japan.

In Germany, after the war, there was a shortage of labourers. I discussed with German officials in Bonn the possibility of sending Barbadian labourers to Germany to help with the labour shortage. The German government was actually thinking of bringing in people from China and Taiwan, but the German minister with whom I spoke told me the big question was housing.

In the 1960s, some parts of Italy still had a labour shortage. I was told both in Rome and in Naples that there would be tremendous room for maids and cooks and that category of worker among certain classes. I discussed it on the floor of the House in Barbados and the Leader of Government business opposed it. Barrow said that Barbadian women would only go up there and become prostitutes.

Shortly after the war ended, I encouraged Barbadians to go to England to find work and acquire all the skills they could so that they could develop the country when they came back. I recall when I was Minister for Industry actually inviting the personnel officers of all the leading hotels and restaurants and tea shops (all the big hotel groups, Lyons Tea Shops and large employers of restaurant workers) to Barbados to the Labour Department at Fontabelle where we invited large numbers of Bajans to meet them. They selected people whom they wanted to take back to work with them in England. As a matter of fact, I was going through the kitchen of the London Hilton one afternoon with the wife of the owner of the land on which the Hilton was built, and somebody said, 'Hi! Mr Crawford.' There were people there from St Philip washing dishes. England had been recruiting small numbers for London Transport before that, and a few nurses were going up at the time, so I made it my business in the early sixties to get people for the hotel and catering industries.

My visit to Panama had nothing to do with sending people there to work. I was actually on a visit to New York, around the mid-1940s, when I got a letter from the West Indian Association in Panama under the signature of the Secretary, Mr Henry Shackleton, inviting me to Panama to discuss problems with the West Indian descendants of immigrants to Panama who had gone there to assist in building the Canal. These people were having trouble with the government of Panama under President Arias. I told him that I could not handle it immediately because I was in New York, but that I would come as early as possible in the New Year.

Early in the following year, the Association sent me a return ticket and I went to Panama to meet and have discussions with them. Apparently, the problem was that the number of descendants of the old immigrants were increasing to such an extent that they could have influenced the results of both the municipal and national elections, both in Panama City and Colon – the other city on the Pacific. Arias was contemplating introducing legislation to disenfranchise not only the original immigrants but also their descendants. There were other problems too.

The night after my arrival we had a general meeting with the entire Association, and then we got down to business with the executive shortly afterwards, to discuss in more detail the problems they were having. I think

I spent about a month in Panama and, eventually, I spoke with the Panamanian government officials and was helped to a great extent by a black female member of the Panamanian Assembly who was very useful in introducing me to the different officials. I talked with the British Ambassador to Panama and had a few interviews with him. Eventually, I produced a report for submission to the British Foreign Office containing recommendations which, if implemented, would rectify the situation and solve the problems the West Indians were having in Panama.

Chief among the recommendations was the appointment of a special advisor to the Ambassador on West Indian Relations to deal with problems of West Indians in Panama. There were other recommendations, of course, the details of which I do not recall. I am happy to say that the British Foreign Office accepted my recommendation and appointed a Jamaican, Henry Morgan. He was appointed to the Embassy to deal specially with West Indian affairs.

The Jamaicans comprised the largest number of West Indian immigrants in Panama. I know that a Barbadian, Cecil Smith, who was originally a reporter for the *Advocate*, (his father was an undertaker in Constitution Road) was in Panama and that he got Morgan's job after his term expired.

Conditions improved considerably after my visit. The embassy officials used to lean over backwards to assist the West Indians after that. The British embassy had been mainly concerned with matters affecting British shipping and trade and any difficulties with British people who were working on the ships going through the canal. But they had had very little interest in any problems of West Indians in Panama itself.

Even before I entered the House of Assembly, I was profoundly concerned with the question of land ownership in Barbados. More than two-thirds of the entire arable acreage was in the hands of a few planters and sugar industrialists. The remainder was divided between the peasants and other smallholders.

I remember the case of a man called Gordon Rose. He had estates in St Thomas – Dunscombe, Content, Welchman Hall and Dukes. These adjoined the estates owned by the Mahons, who were at Lion Castle and Vaucluse. The Mahons reportedly refused to allow Rose to use a road on their place to bring out his canes. It is alleged that Rose threatened them saying, 'Well, you won't let me use the road, I am going to put niggers in your front yard.' He cut up Welchman Hall and sold it to small people. That is why Welchman Hall is such a big agricultural district now. For all that, he had a very bad reputation. It was said that sometimes the labourers would not work for more than two or three days a week, so he had the breadfruit trees cut down because, he said, as long as the workers could get breadfruit they did not have to work.

At the end of the crop, it was customary for the big plantation owners to go to England and come back before the next crop started. They used to call it 'going home'. Even some of the coloured people, when they could muster enough money, took a trip to England and jokingly said they were 'going home' too. When the war broke out, quite a number of Barbadian sugar people were in England vacationing. It was said that Gordon Rose had not intended going in 1939 because he had so much trouble with the workers cutting the canes that year. He went, however, and was in England when the war started. He tried to get home as fast as possible and was travelling on the 'Simon Bolivar', which was one of the first ships torpedoed in the Atlantic. He and his wife perished. I was in the House of Assembly and I immediately called on the government (in 1940) to acquire his plantations and cut them up for land settlement schemes for the agricultural workers. The resolution was tabled in the House. The Mahon group took over his estates finally.

One of the burning desires of the people who emigrated was to buy a piece of land on which to build a house when they returned. My visit to Panama was mainly dealing with problems presented by the Panamanian government but the Barbadians were especially interested in discussing my proposals for land ownership reform in Barbados.

Members of the Barbadian Progressive Society in Panama actually came here between 1941–43 and bought five plantations – Colleton, Lascelles, Prospect, Trents and Four Hills. The man who handled the arrangements was Percy George Seales. There were two brothers who were big land-owners in St James. One of them was buying up land for sale to Panamanians. His brother complained about this, and his reply was, 'You go on planting sugar cane; I am planting Negroes.'

When I was in Panama in 1947, I did not hear of any conflict concerning these estates, so matters must have been going well then. The Society had invested over £60,000. It seems that all the plantations finally ended up in Chancery because of problems with administration. It was a great tragedy that this venture was so disastrous, because the Bajan immigrants in Panama were so interested in the land settlement scheme and desperately wanted to come home and own some land.[2]

Notes

[1]   Adams may have scoffed at the proposal in an aside. According to *Legislative Debates*, Adams did not speak to the resolution, and no one spoke in opposition to it on 30 March 1943.

[2]   The actual sum paid for the five plantations was £52,700. The issue of the ownership of these plantations is still unresolved, mainly because it has apparently proven difficult to identify the descendants of the original members of the friendly society. These properties are administered by a Receiver appointed by the Court of Chancery.

CHAPTER 12

Inside The Democratic Labour Party

ontrary to general belief, Errol Barrow did not start the
Democratic Labour Party. When the DLP started, he was in the
Barbados Labour Party. The DLP was started in 1955 by Owen T. Allder
and L.B. Brathwaithe and one or two others who were disaffected with
Adams. They started meeting at Tudor's house, 'Lemon Grove'. After
Cameron Tudor and Barrow broke with Adams, they went along with
this little group. They met at Tudor's house because they had nowhere
else to meet.[1]

I was getting into my car in the Public Buildings yard one day when
Barrow came to me and said, 'I have just come back from Antigua, and
Vere Bird told me that the DLP will never get anywhere unless Crawford
is in it. If, in order to come in, you want to lead it, I am quite willing to
let you lead.' I said, 'I had nothing to do with the founding of your Party,
and I have no ambition to lead it either. I will work under you but under
nobody else.' So I joined the party. That was in 1956. The place that the
DLP eventually got in Roebuck Street was given to them by James A.
Tudor. He had a seat on the party executive, and I was very annoyed
that, at the very first annual general meeting, they thanked him for the
building and then took him off the Executive Committee. I got up and
made a stinking row. I said, 'How the devil can you expect to thank the
gentleman for giving us somewhere to meet and then boot him off the
Executive Committee!' They put him back on. They continued to meet

Owen T. Allder

there for a long time until they bought the building in Belleville where Dr. Gibbons had his office.

After Barrow and Tudor left Adams, they came over to the Opposition and used to vote in the House of Assembly with Brancker, Talma, "Homie" Corbin and myself. That made six of us. So Barrow did not join us as a leader at all. At the beginning of the session, I said to Brancker, 'Brancks, you can have the leadership. I don't want it personally. I am only dealing with Adams to begin with and you were in the House before me, so go ahead.' So he was the Opposition Leader. Unless he had proved to be incapable, most people would expect, and he would have expected, that if we won the election in 1956, he would have been the leader. He did not have the political personality or the charisma that Barrow had, and during the campaign Barrow did demonstrate more leadership qualities than Brancker. Nevertheless, the correct thing to do would have been to offer him the Premiership if we had won.

James A. Tudor

Colonialism did not breed national leadership. This does not mean that it did not breed a lot of leadership talent, but quite a few of those who became colonial leaders at one time or another had been in England. The British Labour Party was basically anti-colonialist and these colonial students got involved with Labour Party personnel. The Labour Party had endorsed the doctrine that the only way to destroy the power of the Conservatives at home was to weaken them in the colonies because the colonies contributed basically to their wealth and power. So prominent British Labourites indoctrinated a lot of colonial students and they became very strongly anti-colonial when they came back. Also, a number of West Indian students joined the Communist Party in England which preached the same doctrine. Take for example, Michael Manley, Forbes Burnham and Errol Barrow – all were at the London School of Economics with Harold Laski who was very anti-colonial. The average colonial who had not been exposed to the left wing people in England was not likely to be as forthright in the struggle against colonialism as those who had been.

James Cameron (Sir James) Tudor

In the 1956 election Barrow lost his seat in St George. This was partly because at a meeting held outside Government House, as is well known, he proclaimed that masons, carpenters and others of a similar rank would be put on the Legislative Council if the DLP won the election. After that, he ran for a Federal seat and failed. He ran for the St Michael Vestry and failed again. I suggested to him that he should try running in the by-election in St John when V.B. Vaughan was elected to the Federal Legislature. When it was decided that he should contest the seat, I was the person who took him to the parish.

I should mention, in passing, that I had a personal link with St John as well. My father had an aunt who lived in a nice little cottage opposite St John's Boys' School.

Wynter Crawford, Cabinet Minister

Errol Walton Barrow

She was called Mrs Garth and had two daughters, Lily and Rose. One was the headmistress at St Margaret's and played the organ in the church. The other was headmistress at St Mark's and was the organist in that church. When I was a boy, I spent part of my vacation up there.

In later years, this struck me as an example of the rapid progress Negroes had made in Barbados after emancipation. My father was born in 1878 and was the last of five or six children. His mother must have been over thirty when he was born, which means that she was born in the 1840s, and Mrs Garth, her sister, was older and therefore would have been born at the end of slavery. My grandmother (my father's mother) always seemed to me to have a faraway look in her eyes that I never could fathom. I expect that she was always looking back at some dark secret or something, perhaps because her parents would have been slaves.

The people in St John regarded me as their representative. In most districts, they used to come to me with their complaints. I was instrumental in getting uniforms, rubber boots and special clothing for workers in the pumping stations. Once there was some big trouble with the tenantry at Rosegate, and they called me to get it resolved for them.

One Sunday morning I arranged to take Cameron Tudor and Barrow to St John to introduce Barrow to the parish. They were to collect me at my house at 8 a.m. I did not see them till 11 a.m. I said, 'What the devil were you all doing so long?' Cameron said, 'Oh, I was

Frank Leslie (Sir Frank) Walcott

Frank Walcott at Public Meeting

cooking. I have a big basket of food in the back of the car. I couldn't leave home without that.' I said, 'But we should have been in the parish ever since.' (Cammie was a great culinary artist, as is well known.)

I used to campaign with Barrow in St John at night, and every morning Barrow's wife (Carolyn) would ring me to find out how we were doing. After the three previous failures, she did not want him to fail again. I would say, 'Not to worry, he will make it.'

The second island-wide disturbance in the sugar industry took place in 1958 – the year of the by-election in St John. There was an unexpected increase in the price for sugar, what they call a windfall. Every year, the price for sugar, whatever it was, was a negotiated price by the government and I used to publish it in my newspaper and used all the facts and figures I could get. I would announce what price I thought should be paid for peasant farmers' canes and what effect that price would have on the wages for agricultural work. I was once told by Ulric Grant, in connection with the Workers' Union, that they used to wait until they saw what I said before they started negotiating with the industrialists. In 1958 the workers were completely dissatisfied with the price announced both for small farmers' canes and for wage increases. By this time, the

Barbados Workers' Union had a substantial number of agricultural workers among its membership and, completely unauthorized by the Union, the agricultural workers went on strike.

I went through the pickets and I realized they had a case. I went to St Philip and had a meeting because I thought they were right to withhold their labour. By then, I had just joined the Democratic Labour Party and the first Executive meeting we had after the strike started was held in Barrow's Chambers in James Street with Charlie Broomes in the chair. I told them point blank that we had a right to interfere in the strike and support the workers regardless of whether the Union authorised the strike or not; but I could not get them to agree at all. Barrow told me one night that the planters in St John had told him point blank that if he went into that strike they would not give him any votes in the impending by-election. The debate went on for three or four nights with me arguing all the time that we should support the workers. The last night, about 12.00 p.m., I went down the staircase. I said, 'I don't care what the hell you are all doing; I intend to hold a meeting in Queen's Park next Saturday and invite my people in St Philip to come down, as well as people from other parts of the island.' Edwy Talma was there and he got up and said, 'Well, if Crawford is holding a meeting, I am joining him,' and he walked down the stairs behind me. The next morning, about 6.00 a.m., Barrow called by telephone and said that he was at 'T.T.' Lewis's house, and 'T.T.' had told him I was right and that they were damn fools not to support me in it. He said he would join me all day on Saturday. I immediately advertised the meeting in Queen's Park and the whole party was there – Charlie Broomes, Tudor, Barrow, everybody. We all spoke in support of what the workers were doing and agreed to support them until the strike was over. They finally got the increase they wanted.

Shortly after that, the campaign was started for the by-election. I went one morning to Bowmanston pumping station. I knew all the workers there because I had done a lot of work at the various pumping stations to improve their conditions of labour. I talked to the men there and asked them what they thought of our chances of landing Barrow in St John because we were running him against J.W.B. Chenery, a retired police magistrate, and also against Owen T. Allder. Chenery was the Labour Party candidate. So I used the workers at the pumping station as a sort of a gauge. They said, 'At Bowmanston, Mr Crawford, you need not worry at all because St John will support your party because you assisted the workers in that strike when the Union did not authorise it.' Barrow won the by-election.

Wynter Crawford, H.A. Vaughan and Errol Barrow

As the Party prepared for the 1961 election, there was much talk about drafting the manifesto and that it was to be a good one, but nothing was done about it. One Sunday, it was decided to rent a house at Bathsheba, spend the day down there, and some of us would draft the manifesto. We spent the whole day chatting and sea-bathing and, about 6 p.m., Barrow said to me, 'Let us start the manifesto business now.' Everyone else objected. I told them I would draft something and present it to a small group for review at Tudor's house in a few days. When I did, Brancker, Talma, and Tudor reviewed it and thought it was excellent. Barrow came late and, after he had read it, he said, 'This is terrific. All we need is to get some money to have it printed properly.' The only paragraphs in the manifesto which I did not write myself were the paragraphs on education and a small paragraph on constitutional reform. It was circulated and everyone said it played a great part in helping us to win the election. It was agreed that, if we won, Brancker would be Premier.

During the campaign, it is true, Brancker did not play the part that Barrow did. He used to confine himself mostly to his constituency whereas Barrow went with us all over the island. But, for all that, Barrow had not emerged to the point where the public of necessity regarded him as leader. He had only been back in the Assembly for approximately two years and, when he asked me to join the party, he had offered me the leadership.

During the campaign, a meeting was held in Church Village and a man called Grandison or Granville, who worked with the St Michael Highway Commissioners, got up and said that, if the DLP won, they would make Barrow Premier, which was not true. The next morning Brancker rang me about 6 a.m. He said, 'You heard what happened? What are you going to do about it?' I replied, 'Man, I have been studying this very carefully. It appears to me we are going to win, and one of the reasons why we have been doing so well is the fact that there is a lot of squabbling for leadership on the other side – Miller, Cox, Mapp – nobody wants this one or that one. It is easy for us to hold a meeting tomorrow night and for me to say that we have decided to make you Premier. But if I do that, we will lose the election because people will say, 'Both parties are squabbling over the leadership. We had better put back the party that we know.' He said, 'That is a point of view that I can't really ignore, but I will never work under Barrow. If you go along with it, I will be Speaker of the House.'

Sometime afterwards, Elton Mottley told me that his father (Ernest D. Mottley) had told him that he was the person who told Grandison to do it. Elton and I decided that Ernest Mottley paid dearly for it, because it was on account of Mottley that Barrow destroyed the system of local government. As long as local government lasted, you could not beat Mottley in the City or St Michael. These seats were vital and, apart from that, Mottley had some influence throughout the island because of what he did in the St Michael Vestry and in the Corporation of Bridgetown. The fight between Mottley and Barrow over the Mayoralty of Bridgetown, when we had a Mayor and Corporation, was a historic battle. Night after night the two of them were at each other's throats. At one time the Conservatives agreed to run with Mottley in a party called the Mottley Party. I do not know anybody in contemporary politics who controlled a municipality in the way Mottley controlled the metropolitan area. The only way to get rid of Mottley was to destroy the municipality. People in Barbados knew this and some went so far as to say its abolition killed Mottley because he died a short time afterwards.[2]

Mottley, like Barrow and Adams, had the ambition for power and an urge for leadership. I would say I never had it. Brancker, who was at one time Leader of the Opposition and was my deputy in the Congress Party, did not have any special thirst for power either. He wanted to remain in the House as long as he could and he worked with the people in St Lucy to keep himself there. He actually served for thirty-four unbroken years. Some people, however, glory in the quest for power.

Erskine Ward, Errol Barrow and H.A. Vaughan

Yet, I had a lot of friends and people who grew up with me and who shared discussions with me. I always wondered how the devil they could live in a community and die without having made any contribution to it, or without having made any mark on their generation. My own idea was: let me get certain things done. As I went along, I saw more things that I wanted done. I wanted my generation to know that I lived during this time and that I did these things.

A younger brother, Seon, used to work in the Highways Department as a road engineer. One day he was inspecting a highway in Spooner's Hill outside Adams's house and, as Adams was cutting his hedge he told my brother, 'You know, we could never understand how your brother agreed to work with Barrow. That was the surprise of Barbados.' My brother told me about it some time afterwards, and I figured Adams was just trying to make mischief.

On the night when we won the election in 1961, I did not get home until nearly 1 a.m. from St Philip. My mother met me with the news that Barrow had been calling me all night and wanted me to come down to his house in Black Rock as soon as I got in. I told my mother that I was too tired and wanted to go to sleep. She insisted that I should go, so I decided to take her advice. I had to go down to Black Rock from Christ Church and, when I got to Barrow's house, I was surprised to find a number of people in there drinking. Only the night before at our last meeting many of them had been raising hell and saying that we could

not beat Adams. Barrow himself was downstairs in a room with Cameron
Tudor and Tony Vanterpool – giving Tony an interview for the *Advocate*
next day. I was flabbergasted at some of the things that they were saying.
Barrow was rehashing all that stuff about putting masons and carpenters
in the Legislative Council. Only that morning the *Advocate* had reprinted
from the *London Times* a release Adams had given, saying that, if we got
in, the country would be handled by a group of inexperienced and
irresponsible people. I thought, 'Lord, have mercy! he is leading somebody
to say that what Adams had said was true.' So I said, 'Look, Tony, go
home. Everybody is too tired to talk to you properly tonight. Tomorrow
we will give you a proper interview for the *Advocate*.' So Tony left.

Barrow then said to me, 'Now we have won, what does Brancker
want?' I told him that Brancker said he would not dream of working
under him but that he would become Speaker, and that I had offered it
to him. Barrow said, 'If you promised him, he can have it.' Then he said,
'What does Frank Walcott want?' I told him that I had discussed it with
Frank Walcott and he had said that he did not want a Ministry because
he was going to stick to the Union. (The story was that he had broken
with Adams because he had not been given a ministry.[3])

I knew that neither Barrow nor Tudor had much experience in
government, so I said to Barrow, 'I think we ought to have another
experienced person in the Cabinet, somebody that would give it a certain
semblance of maturity.' He said, 'Do you have anybody in mind?' I said,
'Hilton Vaughan.' He said, 'Vaughan and I don't get along. I can't have

*Members of DLP Cabinet (front row from left): DaCosta Edwards, George Ferguson,
Cameron Tudor, Edwy Talma, H.A. Vaughan. (Back row from left): Errol Barrow,
the Governor Sir John Stowe, Wynter Crawford.*

him.' Several times before I had approached Vaughan, asking him to leave the civil service because he was not getting promoted since his clash with Adams and suggesting that he could run for the House and get in for St Philip. He had always refused, and the last time I went to his house asking him to run, his wife met me in the Public Buildings yard afterwards and told me that she did not want him to get mixed up in politics again and, if he ran, she would divorce him. However, I told Barrow, 'You don't mind that. I can get him.' So I left Black Rock that night and went straight to Vaughan's house and woke him up. When I told him why I had come, he said, 'Me? Me and that sod don't get along. Every time he comes in my court, he is damn rude and I promised to send him up for contempt next time he does it.' I said, 'Forget all that, man.' He finally accepted, and I rang to tell Barrow. The next morning he went to Vaughan's house to thank him, and then he came to see me and thanked me for getting him.

Later, in 1963, when Erskine Ward came back from Trinidad, I told Barrow that he would be missing something if he did not use Erskine, a man of terrific ability with a lot to offer. He 'hemmed' and 'hawed' because he did not know very much about Erskine. When Erskine was offered something in the city, I told him that, if he did not get him then, he would lose him. Eventually he brought him into the Cabinet as Minister without Portfolio. Afterwards, Barrow told someone I knew that he had never met a man with such universality of knowledge.

Ceremonial Opening of Parliament 1961; J.E.T. Brancker, Speaker (in official robes) and Wynter Crawford (in glasses) third after Speaker

At the first meeting of the Cabinet when we met with Barrow as Premier, his first question was, 'Well gentlemen, where do we go from here?' He addressed the question to me. I said, 'Well, the first thing we have to do, since we raised this question of unemployment so strongly during the campaign, is to put people to work. We are going to start the East Coast Road first, which I have been clamouring for since 1942–43, nearly twenty years ago. We are going to do some work at the airport, and we are going to drain the Constitution Swamp which has been long ago in the Congress manifesto.' Adams had opposed the draining of the Constitution Swamp after large crowds had collected outside my office asking me to hold a meeting and call Adams a murderer after the flooding of the Constitution River (in August 1949) had endangered life and property. We started from there with the crash programme and the impetus we gained then carried us through for a long, long time.

One difficulty we faced was the island-wide unrest in the sugar industry in 1963/64 over the sugar 'windfall' issue. In 1963 we sold a certain amount of sugar on the British market at a negotiated price, and what was left could be sold anywhere at the prevailing world price. During the war, we had arranged to sell a portion of our sugar production to Britain at a price far below what we would have got for it in the world market then. In return for this, Britain promised that after the war, she would still continue to take a fixed amount of the production at a negotiated price. Every year we sent a man up there, Sir Archibald Cuke, to negotiate the price. That year we sold the extra amount of sugar to Nigeria and got a lot of money. The workers decided that the share allotted to them was inadequate and refused to cut the canes. I was Minister of Labour at the time and, one Monday morning, two armed workers went into my house and demanded to see me immediately because they could not understand why I did not authorise the government to resolve the issue between themselves and the sugar industrialists. Thereafter, the government ordered armed guards for Frank Walcott, Barrow and myself. We had armed policemen guarding our homes. There was a big increase in the price of sugar and the sugar industrialists got their share but the Union considered that the part belonging to the workers should not be given to the workers but to the Union. Apparently, the Union wanted this money to make a fund which would guarantee the pensions for Union officers when they retired. I felt that the Union members paid their subscriptions and these subscriptions should be used to defray all the expenses of the Union, so I never went along with this at all.

Of course I was overruled. This was the first issue of contention between Barrow and myself. Both he and Frank Walcott knew my stand on the matter, and Frank was telling everybody that, if I had agreed, the Union would have got the money without any trouble at all. I forgot how many million dollars it was but my contention was that, if the sugar industrialists got their share of the money, there was no reason at all why the workers should not get their share individually. The Union's attitude was, 'what were the workers going to do with all that money?' I thought they could buy a fridge or a stove or some luxury they could not afford before.

I know that early in this century, when Joseph Chamberlain was Colonial Secretary, the sugar industry in the West Indies was at a very low ebb and he got the British government to give a grant to the West Indian sugar producers. Each island got a share. Barbados, so far as I remember, got £80,000. They called the Chamberlain Bridge after him, and the sugar planters in Barbados, unlike the sugar planters in the other West Indian colonies, took that money and founded a bank known as the Sugar Industry Agricultural Bank, and that money was used for years to maintain and support the sugar industry. I was a Director of both that bank and the Peasants' Loan Bank. I was on the Board when they appointed Noel Symmonds as a Director of the Sugar Industry Agricultural Bank but, before that, we had appointed a man called Bethell as Assistant Manager. He belonged to the minor planter class. There were a lot of big sugar people as Directors of the Bank. They were white in those days, of course. They were bitterly opposed to Bethell because he got to know all the planters' business.

I remember when the manager retired and we appointed Bethell as Manager. Some of the white members threatened to resign. The same thing happened when we wanted to appoint Symmonds as Assistant Manager because no coloured man had ever been in the bank before.

That £80,000 grant from the British government really served the sugar industry well. I suppose the idea behind the Union's claim was that, in the same way that this bounty was used to service the industry, the workers' share of the bounty that year should have been used for the Union to invest. But the workers did not agree because it was their money and they wanted it in their hands – and I went along with them. The Barbados Labour Party was holding meetings – Allder and Brathwaite also were holding meetings – night after night, and they felt they were right in opposing the DLP government, and they told the workers to keep up the demand until they got their share. Eventually the government had to give in.

Subsequently the Union did get a large amount of money from the government for this purpose. They got it in the year of the Constitutional Debates when the government authorized a certain amount of the reserve funds from the sugar industry to be given to the planters and a certain amount to the Union.

In 1963, I never agreed to withholding the money at all. I was the Minister of Labour and I did not hold any meetings or anything like that, but the whole island knew that I did not support it. Frank Walcott knew, and I do not think he will ever forgive me for it. Barrow and the whole party knew. This led to serious problems inside the Cabinet but not openly. My Cabinet colleagues were just annoyed that I did not go along with them but they could not fault me on that at all.

Notes

1   The official history of the DLP indicates that two 'tributaries' of protest met to form the party. One tributary, the older, was led by Allder and Brathwaite, while the newer one was led by parliamentarians, disaffected members of the Barbados Labour Party – Errol Barrow, A.E.S. Lewis, F.G. Smith, and Cameron Tudor. Discussions between the two groups from February to April 1955 ended in agreement to launch a political party which would be both democratic and socialist.

2   E.D. Mottley died in 1973, six years after local government had been abolished.

3   Frank Leslie (Sir Frank) Walcott (1916–1998), National Hero of Barbados, was an internationally acclaimed trade unionist and a highly influential political figure in Barbados. As General Secretary of the Barbados Workers' Union from 1948 to 1991, he was mainly responsible for its emergence, particularly after 1954, as a disciplined, effective, comprehensive and **independent** organization. In 1954 he led the union into a breakaway from its sister organization, the Barbados Labour Party; and he himself was identified with the Democratic Labour Party from 1956 to 1976. He sat in the House of Assembly from 1945 to 1966 and again from 1971 to 1976.

CHAPTER 13

Promoting Industrial Development

They talk a lot about industries now, but for years I was the only person in Barbados talking about the necessity for embarking upon an industrial development campaign. The first industrial incentive in the early 1940s was due to me and involved a company called West Indies Knitting Mills. I had already introduced a resolution in the House of Assembly, based on the Industrial Incentives Act of Puerto Rico, which Munoz Marin had given me, calling for industrial incentives to attract industries to the island. It took ten years before Adams brought down that Bill. After we passed the legislation to set up what they called the Industrial Development Board, it took another three years before they could find a manager for it.

I was in my office one day and a man called Saunders walked in. He was on a ship going to Trinidad, and he knew a merchant in Swan Street called Feldman. He had gone to him and told him that he was an industrialist and would like to put an industry in Barbados but, since the government was not offering the same concessions as Trinidad, he was going to Trinidad. At that time we had quite a wave of Jews fleeing from Hitler and coming to the Caribbean from Poland, Czechoslovakia and Germany, and other European countries. Feldman had said to Saunders, 'The only man in Barbados talking about industry is Crawford. He is around the corner there at Lucas Street. Go and see him.' So Mr Saunders came to me and said he wanted to put a plant here but we offered no incentives

Arawak Cement Factory: a Crawford proposal

at all. He wanted to establish a knitting mill to spin cotton, which he could get from some of the other islands, to make underwear, socks and garments and that sort of product. Instead of going to Trinidad, he would come here if the government would promise him incentives. I said, 'Mr Saunders, you go down to Trinidad and, when you come back, I will see you. Don't do anything there. I will see what I can do in the meantime.' I went to the Colonial Secretary, a man called G.D. Owen, and said, 'Mr Owen, there is an industrialist who has a plant in Jamaica. He wants to put a spinning plant here, and I want to know what the government intends to do about my suggestions for giving industrial incentives to people who want to come in.' He said, 'Oh, we haven't done anything about it, Mr Crawford.' I said, 'I will tell you something; if this man does not get assistance in this direction, I intend to hold an island-wide campaign and attack the government on its laziness and indifference to this question because it is a matter of employing people. I will start from next week and campaign in the city, in Queen's Park.' Owen said, 'Mr Crawford, don't do that. You leave it to me for a few days and I will see what I can do.'

When Saunders came back from Trinidad, I told him that I expected to hear from the Colonial Secretary. And I did, in a few days. He told me to tell Saunders to go ahead and he would see to it that he was granted permission to bring in the equipment duty-free. Saunders was allowed to bring in his equipment duty-free and the Industrial Incentives legislation was passed. Saunders put down a plant near Johnson Stables and he started knitting and spinning cotton from St Vincent and other places. He then moved the plant to Spry Street and since then it has been moved to Wildey near CBC. It employs nearly one hundred people up there still, and has been going on ever since.

I drafted the terms of the resolution for the setting up of a flour mill, and a feasibility study was done demonstrating how it would be of benefit to the country to manufacture flour from imported wheat. The chaff could be used for making animal feeds. I went to Puerto Rico myself, at my own expense, to see the operation of the flour mill there. The Molinos, who were the owners from Puerto Rico, were very kind and they took me all through the plant. They actually had bought a small plantation outside San Juan to experiment with the different kinds of animal feed produced from the chaff from the flour. At that time, Haiti was selling a lot of animal feed here, which came from the chaff from their flour mill. Adams did absolutely nothing about it. We could have had the flour mill very much earlier.

Later, when I was Minister of Development, I actually concluded arrangements with a Chinese flour miller from Hong Kong to establish a mill here. This was years before the present one was put down. I had been advertising and had tried all sorts of Canadian flour mills, but I did not get correct assistance because they wanted to keep the market for their flour. When I started talking about the flour mill in Barbados, Adams got up at a meeting one night and said that I was talking damn nonsense because the Canadian government would never allow a flour mill to be started in Barbados because they were depending on Barbados for marketing their flour.

The father and grandfather of this Chinese miller had flour mills in China before Mao ran them out. They also had mills in Singapore, Hong Kong and elsewhere. He came down to Barbados sometime in the early 1960s and came to the Ministry to see me. He said that he had seen the notice that we wanted a flour miller. C.B. 'Boogles' Williams, my Permanent Secretary, and myself went through all the stuff about what incentives and what assistance he would get from the government including a guaranteed market. He left to start to work on the project but, within a few months of his return to Hong Kong, he took very ill with a serious heart attack and could no longer go through with the project.

It was the same thing with the cement plant. I had been talking about both grey and white cement – because we have deposits here which are

East Coast Road: another Crawford proposal

suitable for the production of white cement. The government never took any notice of it at all. When I was in government myself, I tried several countries to get a plant that would produce for our requirements economically, but we discovered that our consumption was not large enough to warrant the construction of the sort of plant we could get. I discovered that there was a small plant in Switzerland which would supply our requirements economically. Vere Bird then came along with the plan for the Federation of 'the Little Eight'. This could have created a much larger market and would have enabled us to benefit from producing cement on a much larger scale. We were working on it and we already had nearly a hundred applicants wanting to establish industries in Barbados. Barbados would have been the headquarters for the 'Little Eight', and would have had their combined population to make any operation economically feasible. When the Federation talks broke up, this was no longer possible.

After the proposal for the federation of the 'Little Eight' fell through, the government came up with Caricom. The basic reason behind Caricom at the time was to make up for the fact that we had thrown away the federation of the 'Little Eight'. Barbados was to have been the government headquarters and would have been the industrial centre for the 'Little Eight' because the other islands had no secondary industries capable of maintaining equipment in good condition as we had. We had the Barbados Foundry, Central Foundry and such places. There was nothing like this in the Leeward and Windward Islands. So we would have been the centre for the industries. I had always said that we would not want to retain all the big industries for ourselves. But certain industries could be set up in those islands which produced the raw materials which would make industry feasible. Once I made a number of enquiries about different industries that could be developed from using coconuts, and I heard that in Ceylon they had a number of industries making rope and matting from the coconut fibres. I spoke to the Ceylonese embassy in London and they gave me quite a lot of information.

Norman Manley did a lot for Jamaica in terms of social welfare and handicraft industries and domestic utilization of Jamaican raw materials. Even before the DLP got into power, I had been trumpeting these ideas about expanding the economy of the country. As soon as the DLP got in, Barrow and I had to go on a visit to New York and I told him that my plan was to go on to Mexico. He said that he would come along because Mexico had led the way towards the economic development of what was known as the under-developed countries in a manner that no other country had done. From the beginning, as far back as the 1920s, the Mexican president – Cardenas – had nationalized the oil industry. He then began to industrialize Mexico and, added to that, he expanded cottage industries, as a result of which Mexico became well-known for the diversification of cottage industries. When we enquired at the embassy in Washington (this was late December, early January) the staff there told us that there was no point in going then because all the government authorities in Mexico were on holiday from Christmas until almost the end of January. So we did not go. Barrow went there subsequently, because I saw it published in the newspaper, but I never did.

The fact that Mobil Oil in Barbados is still operating is due entirely to me because they were on the brink of closing down. Frank Walcott had been trying for years to get increased wages for the workers. Mobil Oil was sending home men all the time and the management claimed that it was no longer possible to keep the plant going. When I was Minister of Trade and Industry, a conflict developed between Mobil and the Union because Mobil wanted to retrench more workers. I went into the matter with Mobil very carefully and I decided that something had to be done about it. Eventually I proposed to the government that Mobil should be given the rights and privileges to process all the crude oil that was required for Barbados. Aviation fuel could not be manufactured here, so therefore we would continue to import it. There was a hell of a hue and cry by the other suppliers of gas like Texaco and Shell. They wanted to crucify me but I insisted that it was the correct thing to do in giving Mobil the rights.

Crawford as Minister of Industry with visiting industrialists

Barrow agreed, and he and I went to New York and talked to Mobil about it. They were very grateful for the suggestion because they were on the verge of closing down. As I pointed out then, we were importing petroleum products from Trinidad. Trinidad itself could not supply the raw material for its refineries and was importing additional crude from the Far East, the Middle East and Venezuela, and was then supplying us with refined oil. So Trinidad was very opposed to it. I saw that if we needed crude that we should import it ourselves and expand Mobil. So Mobil was expanded and given some assistance and they are still operating now. 'Boogles' Williams, my Permanent Secretary, was with me at the time. I proposed it and we worked on it and submitted it to Cabinet.

There was a tremendous amount to be learned from the Mexican handicraft and cotton industries. When Woolworth wanted to put a business in Mexico City, the Mexican government at the time refused to allow them to establish it unless 90% of what they were going to market was manufactured in Mexico. I was in London a year or two after that when I met Lord Morris, the head of Morris Motors. I was there on an industrial trip. He invited me to come down to Birmingham to talk to the Birmingham Chamber of Commerce and see what industries I could induce to come to Barbados. He said to me, 'There is something I am very proud of. You know that scheme in Mexico to be industrially self-sufficient?' I said, 'Yes, I've heard about it.' He said, 'Well, they have selected six world-wide motor car manufacturers to establish plants in Mexico to produce cars, and they are putting very prohibitive tariffs against imported cars.

They have invited General Motors, Vauxhall, Volkswagen, Mercedes, and Morris is among them. So that means that we should be putting a plant in Mexico City for Morris and Austin. We have to supply Central America from there as well.' So Barbados had a lot to learn from Mexico. I never did go, but I thought we could have had talks with the Mexican Chamber of Commerce and the Manufacturers' Association, and in the spin-off something would have been done for industries and cottage industries in Barbados.

Ground-Breaking for Pelican Industrial Estate

I had been thinking about Japan and Hong Kong and trying to see what we could learn from their situation. There was a firm called Little & Co., an American firm that did industrial surveys. Between 1961 and 1962, I contracted this company, to make a survey of Barbados and come up with ideas of the kinds of industries they thought would be economically feasible for Barbados with maximum utilization of local raw material. There was also a Japanese firm in New York which did the same thing. When 'Bree' St John took office, I gave him the literature on it. But the thing was to bring the representative of the firm to Barbados to make a survey of what industries he thought could be established here and then we would send a delegation with him to Japan to invite the appropriate industrialists there to come back here and talk business. These are things that I had explored thoroughly. Barrow went to Japan with F.L. Cozier, who was Permanent Secretary, and I understand he went to Japan twice. We never heard one thing about anything they did. Since then, 'Bree' St John has gone to Japan and we have begun to see some results of what he went for, because he has revived the cotton industry. We are up to a point now of exporting cotton to Japan.

Once when I was in London, I had discussions with Anthony Murray, Director of the West India Committee. The British cotton industry was not competitive because the Egyptians produced the long staple which was the best cotton in the world. In the West Indies, Sea Island cotton

Crawford Visiting Factory on Industrial Estate

was the second best. Many of the cotton spinners in Manchester and Lancaster were closing down, and I was suggesting that what they should do was to bring some of the equipment down here to spin the cotton instead of our sending the raw material up there all the time. I am glad to see that we have started with cotton again because, if we start producing enough, we need not only sell raw material to Japan but we can start doing some spinning down here in the West Indies.

We were doing a little smocking here when the DLP took office and I thought that it should be expanded, so when I was in New York I searched around until I found the America National Embroiderers' Association and met with its Director, Albert Gilman. I invited him to Barbados to see what we had been doing in the Handicraft Centre. He came down with another colleague and his wife, and he thought we needed a lot of improvements. He kindly agreed to my suggestion that I should send four of the girls who were working in the Centre together with the Director of the Social Welfare Department, Miss Marjorie Blackman, to New York, to be taught American methods of production so that they could come back here and teach the other girls in the island. This was done and we have been able to do quite a lot with the embroidery for export and extend its possibilities.

It was the considered opinion of many that, unlike Adams, Barrow was a lawyer who was receptive to ideas. He followed along with any suggestions for industrial improvement or anything like that and was prepared to give credit to the party for whatever was achieved. Many of the things we had to tackle in 1961 would have been done long before if Adams's mind had been cast in a similar mould.

One or two things Barrow did not go along with. For instance, one was Sunset Crest. That was my idea. I called a meeting in the Ministry and invited a lot of tourist people, the bank managers and hotel people, and told them what I had in mind for Barbados at that stage. I was Minister of Tourism and held several other portfolios at the same time. I said, 'What we need here now is to do what Florida did years ago. We want to attract North Americans down here to live when they retire.' At that time, there was a large number of Americans running down to Florida to build or buy houses to get away from the cold up north. Canadians were doing it too. Sometimes people buying land in Florida could not find it when they got there because it was swamp.

The proposition I put before them was for the construction of about 1,000 homes for retired North Americans to come down here and live. Their friends and families would come and visit them. They would spend their pensions and income here, and I estimated at the time that this would have contributed about $20,000,000 per year to the economy. I figured that, if about 1,000 people came down with a pension of about $10,000 US dollars per year each, they would spend the money in addition to what money they had before and employ chauffeurs, cooks and maids and other staff. The construction of the houses would entail a lot of money and a lot of work. It was unanimously agreed that it was a great idea.

I was in London shortly afterwards with Barrow attending the the 'Little Eight' meeting in Marlborough House and told him, 'When I go back home, I am going to start concentrating on my proposal for homes for retired North Americans.' His answer to me was, 'I wouldn't work on that if I were you. You bring all those Americans down here to live, and people like you or me would not be able to employ any servants or maids. They would pay too much money and we would not be able to compete with them.' I said nothing. At the time, I did not know how to take the statement. When I came back, I did not do anything about it right away, and thought that I should let it rest for a little while because I did not know whether or not he wanted me to do it.

Around that time, a Canadian called Huff had paid down some money on Heywoods plantation and wanted to put a hotel there. He went to the Development Board to borrow some money to assist in establishing his hotel. K.R. Hunte was chairman then. At the time, the Development Board was not allowed to lend more than a certain amount of money without the approval of the Minister in charge. The Board approved the money but, when it came to me, I told the Board that I was opposing it, on the grounds that we had never yet lent so much money to anybody in the hotel industry and, if we were to lend that amount of money, it would have to be to a Barbadian. Huff would have to get his deposit in Canada. Huff was very annoyed, I heard, and said that he would plead with the Prime Minister. Hunte and Huff went down to Barrow about it. So Barrow called me one day and asked me why I refused to lend the money. I told him that Huff was a non-Barbadian. I told him that the most we would lend to any non-Barbadian was $45,000 to $50,000 – a small amount in those days – and he wanted $75,000. If we lent it, it would have to be to a Bajan firm. So Barrow said, 'I'll tell you what I will do. I will call a meeting between us and we will discuss it, you, Hunte, Huff and myself on Saturday morning at 9.00.' I agreed, and on the Saturday morning I went to Barrow's office at 9.00 a.m. but he was not there. Shortly afterwards, Hunte and Huff came in, and Hunte said, 'Is Mr Barrow here?' When he was told that I was the only one there, they left. Barrow never came. So that was that.

The manager of the Development Board, a Mr McClellan, was involved in this business with Hunte. He was to manage the hotel. He had only a three-year contract with the Development Board, so he resigned from the Board and he and Huff went to Canada to try and raise the money. They had all sorts of advertisements in the Canadian papers and could not raise a cent. So some months afterwards while I was sleeping a little late one Sunday morning, there was a knock on the door and I was told that it was Mr McClellan who wanted to see me. I said, 'Mr McClellan? He is supposed to be in Canada.' So I got up and went to him and he said, 'Mr Crawford, I want to ask you a question. You know I live in Canada now, but my wife does not want to live there anymore. She would love to live down here, and she told me that she wanted me to come back down here and find a job.' I said, 'I personally have no objections.' He said, 'I would like to revive that scheme you talked about – a thousand homes for North Americans. It is an excellent idea and I would like to work on it. Do you know anywhere we could get an appropriate site to do it?' I said, 'You know when Ronald Tree bought Sandy Lane estate to put down the Sandy Lane hotel, he bought it from DaCosta and Company who had taken it over from the Thornes and there were one hundred acres left which he said he could not afford to buy then. I believe that DaCosta might be able to come in with you on it. Go and see them.' He said, 'Who should I see at DaCosta's?' I said, 'A man named David Lucie Smith. He handles that kind of thing there.' So he thanked me and left.

The Monday morning about half-past ten he called and said, 'Mr Crawford, I am in business. I went to Lucie-Smith, and DaCostas want to come in with me right away. Alleyne Arthur wants to come in and take a share in it because they would like to get their grocery business down there. I rented a house, called 'Marlborough', opposite Government House, and I have an office in High Street.' I said, 'Good luck! Go ahead.' And McClellan started. He must have collected some money. He said he would build a house or two as an exhibition, so that various people from North America would come down and look at them and advertise them. He had an opening function and he invited me, as the Minister of Tourism, to come down and turn the sod for the erection of the first house. After the two houses were built, applications for houses began coming in from all over the United States. The condition was that a deposit was to be made by the buyer, the house would be built and rented. When the owner was not occupying it, the management rented it throughout the year and credited the owner's account less the cost of expenditures and maintenance. Then, after a while, the house became the property of the owner. But after the scheme began to succeed so well, he twisted the original terms and increased the time it would take to own the house. His houses stopped selling right away. The project never got off the ground. So eventually he must have left the island.

Quite a while afterwards, there was a man here called Alfred Laforet who was a contractor. He had a firm called Building Supplies and he also had a brick factory down in St Andrew making red clay bricks. He called me one morning and said he wanted to see me. He said, 'Mr Crawford, I want to revive your scheme down at Sunset Crest. I would like some details about it. I think it has tremendous possibilities.' So I told him what had happened to McClellan, as far as I knew, and I sent him back down to sound out Lucie-Smith. Laforet was a hell of an entrepreneur. He got help from DaCosta and Lucie-Smith, and he started building the houses down there and selling them. He made a tremendous success of it and then sold it. I do not know who bought it. I have heard that it was the biggest development of its kind in the world – Sunset Crest. The tourist recession in the last couple of years hit it just like everywhere else. Although the scheme was a good idea, it was badly exploited. I know that an American Medical School used it for a time.

I understand that the American authorities are cracking down on some of the off-shore schools in the West Indies. It is likely that most of those students would have wanted to come to study here if the school had been set up in Barbados. So I am told. I talked to one of the students here a few months ago. I think he told me that they pay $400 – $600 per month rent for a cottage which really is a godsend. Without that, the scheme would have had to close down because of the recession in tourism. Sunset Crest was a terrific tourist area and it brought in a lot of money to the island when tourism was doing well. As far as I know, it was bigger than most of the resorts that Club Med has in the Mediterranean. I doubt that they ever got to the 1,000 houses, but I have seen some of the resorts done by Club Med. They were many of them in France and they go right across the Mediterranean, through the Balearic Islands off the coast of Spain right up to Morocco, and Israel has some too. They have got some in the West Indies now in the Bahamas and Martinique. I have seen quite a few of them and they are nothing at all like Sunset Crest. If tourism is revived, the scheme could flourish again and would employ a lot of people. Laforet did a very good job.

In the early stage in the development of tourism, there were a few letters from time to time in the newspapers against the introduction of gambling. Some people also feared that some of the racial prejudice that already existed in Barbados might be aggravated by tourism, but I do not think Adams ever studied the matter carefully. He was not interested in anything like that. We had a Tourist Board at the time, which was doing its best. It included a man called Harry Niblock and Maurice Cave of Cave Shepherd. There is heavy investment in tourism now. The government gives the Tourist Board a small stipend every year and increases it from time to time. Occasionally there was some trouble with the hotels not wanting the locals to use the beaches. Years ago, Dr. Cummins had to put up some resistance to the owners of Paradise Hotel who wanted to refuse permission to people who wanted to use the beach. Once I had some trouble myself with regard to public bathing near the west coast hotels. But there was not anything big to worry about.

CHAPTER 14

Departure From Active Politics

he 'Little Eight' Federation was proposed after Jamaica and Trinidad had seceded from the West Indies Federation. I was in Trinidad attending a conference to fix the price of rice when the announcement was made that Eric Williams had pulled Trinidad out of the Federation with the famous statement that '1 from 10 leaves 0'. Immediately after the Trinidad announcement, the idea of the 'Little Eight' was conceived. I think that Vere Bird, then Premier of Antigua, was the leading agitator for the continuation of a Federation even without Trinidad and Jamaica. As senior representative there, Bird made the public pronouncement of their agreement to go ahead with all the Leewards, Windwards and Barbados to form a Federation. The Secretary of State for the Colonies arranged to have a conference immediately in Trinidad to discuss the proposition. I was asked by Errol Barrow to remain there until he and the other delegates came down. This was in January 1962.

Barrow, Bird, Hilton Vaughan, Sir Arthur Lewis and probably Auguste Pinard were all there. I was a bit sceptical myself in the beginning because the Leewards and the Windwards had been Crown Colonies for a long time and had not had the opportunity that we had in Barbados to practise even the beginning of representative government. I was concerned about what would happen, especially with the parties that were in office then, and the type of parties that might be returned in their places in the islands. But I was willing to discuss the matter. Barrow also had hesitations as well. I

Errol Barrow and Vere Bird,

clearly remember Bird saying, 'Errol, if we go into this grouping, I will see that you become the first Premier.' I did not pay much attention to Bird's statement at first, but Barrow decided immediately to go along.

We agreed to hold a conference in London shortly afterwards to discuss the matter with the British government. Barrow and I represented Barbados and we took along Auguste Pinard, the Financial Secretary to the Governor. It was fortunate that all three of us were staying at the same hotel, the Mount Royal, because it was Pinard who woke me up one morning very early when Barrow became very seriously ill. He had gone upstairs to Barrow's room and found him on the floor twisting and writhing in pain. We called a Barbadian, Dr. Bertie Clarke, a well known West Indian cricketer and medical doctor. When he saw Barrow on the floor, he said it might have been appendicitis. I said, 'No, man, it must be his kidneys because he is holding his back.' In no time we had him rushed to the hospital. That Sunday afternoon, Sir John Stow, the Governor, Pinard and myself went to the hospital. I remember the matron of the hospital saying, 'Your Premier was a very lucky man. There were only two doctors in the whole of England who could have saved his life. One had already left for vacation on the continent for the weekend and the other was about to leave when Dr Clarke stopped him and got him here. He is doing his best for him but, if he were in Barbados, you all would be attending his funeral this evening.' Mrs Barrow came up from Barbados to the hospital in England for a few days. The doctor who saved his life was given a special invitation by the government to attend the Independence celebrations here, and he was given an award.

I remember very well an incident which took place at Marlborough House at the time. In the early part of the proceedings, the British government had suspended the constitution in Grenada and had appointed a Commission to enquire into the alleged misappropriation of funds by the Premier, Eric Gairy. He came to me the afternoon the announcement was made and said, 'Barrow is ill. We accept the fact that you are now leading the West Indian delegation and I want you to call a meeting of all the West Indian delegates immediately.' I said, 'What for, Gairy?' He said, 'The British government can't walk in there and suspend the constitution like that. After all, we have to protest against it. We can't let them ride roughshod over us. I haven't done anything. I would like you to call a meeting this evening of all the delegates and let us pass a resolution telling them to hands off Grenada.' I replied, 'Well, Gairy, I think that, because of the circumstances, the British government has already announced the appointment of this Commission of Enquiry. We should as least await the report of the Commission before we take any action. I agree with you that we cannot allow them to ride roughshod over us, but let us see what the Commission says. They have to report immediately.' Gairy said to me, 'What? You are going to accept the word of the Commission of Enquiry appointed by England against mine? I haven't done anything wrong. All I have done is spend some money on the road – the road to my entrance was very bad and visitors to my house used to complain about it (he lived in the official residence in Grenada). I also spent some in buying a piano for my wife. It is a better piano than the one at Government House. But then my wife was entitled to it because she plays the piano practically every night.' So I said, 'Well Gairy, I stick to my proposal that we await the report of the Commission before we take any such action as you suggest.' Of course, he was highly indignant about it.

After that first conference in London, we gave the delegates a house here in Two-Mile Hill called 'Sherbourne' to hold all the conferences that had to be held to decide on the constitution and all the other things that had to be fixed. We selected Erskine Ward and Hilton Vaughan to represent Barbados and attend all the meetings that were convened there.

By this time, though, I was actually pursuing the programme I had always had in mind and had been talking about for over twenty years – that is, industrialising Barbados. I found that quite a number of schemes that I had envisaged for Barbados were not practical unless we had a larger grouping of people which the Federation would have provided. For instance, I had been talking about a flour mill for a long time but, in actual fact, the population of Barbados alone could not support a flour mill or a cement plant. The smallest cement plant then that could have operated with a degree of financial success would have turned out more cement than Barbados could utilise in a given period, but the population of the Leeward and Windward Islands, added to ours, would have made all these programmes practicable. Furthermore, the other leaders had decided to make Barbados the headquarters of the Federation. All of the embassies and consular offices would have been sited here, and I concluded that, economically, it would have been a great advantage for the country. We had a lot to offer each other in terms of natural resources.

We had certain things that we could have provided to the Leewards and Windwards that they did not have themselves and vice versa. We had decided to earmark certain developments for each island in the Federation. For example, St Lucia could have raised enough sheep and goats to provide for the area and remove the necessity for importing meat. Dominica and St Vincent could have provided certain vegetables and fruit and foodstuffs that we could not provide ourselves, and we in turn could have supplied them with whatever industrial products we produced. There was no place in the Leewards or Windwards which had anything like the Barbados Foundry for repairing machines. We had nearly a hundred applicants who were willing to establish industries in Barbados. I do not remember offhand exactly all of the positive aspects which would have accrued to Barbados from having the headquarters sited here. However, I felt that, provided that the people in those islands had reached a certain standard of political education, the Federation could work.

I had no time to go to 'Sherbourne'. Barrow certainly had no time because, in my opinion, the Cabinet we had was not really very competent. Capt. Ferguson had never been in politics before; we had Joy Edwards who was Minister of Social Welfare. I had been working for years on a programme for National Insurance from the time that the Beveridge Plan was published in England during the war. Churchill had requested Sir William Beveridge (afterwards Lord Beveridge) prepare a National Insurance Plan for Britain, as he said, to take care of people from the cradle to the grave. I prepared a similar plan for Barbados based on the Beveridge Plan, making the necessary adaptations, and presented it on the floor of the House. That was in 1948, but it was ignored.

Barrow came to me one day and said, 'Edwards has had this National Insurance project and has never got it before the Assembly. Since you worked on it for years, work on it for me.' I worked on that document. I was going to a meeting of the ILO after I had finished it, and I asked Erskine to give it to the Cabinet. He did, and later I put it through the House. There was much to be done and the Permanent Secretaries worked well. As a matter of fact, it was generally thought at the time that Carlisle Burton did all the work in his Ministry. Algy Symmonds was also a Permanent Secretary, but Barrow did not care much for those who had been appointed by the Adams government. 'Boogles' Williams was always neutral and worked very hard. He was my Permanent Secretary when I did the National Insurance Scheme and was with me through all the industrial development programmes. Wilfred Rogers also worked very well and eventually became Cabinet Secretary, a post he richly merited.

Most of the work at 'Sherbourne' really fell on Erskine Ward. Hilton Vaughan also assisted. It would have been absolutely impossible for us to send anybody else up there. In any case, we thought that the work was fairly cut and dried since the delegates had the proceedings from the earlier meetings held to formulate the Federation of the West Indies. Some modifications might have been necessary because of the smaller population of the 'Little Eight.' All the material on the Customs Union and the unification of the Civil Service was already there. I do not remember all these chaps now, because I have not been reading any of this for years but, in comparison with the delegates from the other islands, there was nobody there better than Vaughan and Ward.

My understanding is that it was W.H. Bramble who broke up the 'Little Eight'. It seems that, in the final meeting with Barrow, something occurred which annoyed Bramble or probably the delegates, and Bramble got up and said, 'Barrow, you want to treat us like if we are your ministers. Our understanding is that you treat most of your ministers as you like. We are the same leaders as you are, and we have decided that if this Federation goes through we will make Erskine Ward the first Premier. I know that Barrow walked out of the conference in a rage and said, 'I am leaving and after I have left nobody can speak for Barbados but me.'

That evening we went immediately to Erskine Ward's house. We did not discount what he reported. We figured that what he said was gospel truth. I had not tried to make contact with Barrow because I had not heard of the episode with Bramble until then. We really could not understand how, after all the work they had been doing for eighteen months, how after we had placed 'Sherbourne' at the disposal of the delegates and had undertaken to bear all the expenses that were incurred, suddenly Barrow could break up the Conference. We thought it was an insult to all the delegates and to the people of the Eastern Caribbean when he said, 'After I am gone, nobody can speak for Barbados.'

What Bramble had said that he had heard was not entirely incorrect. This would have happened in 1965, but I suppose some of us were already annoyed with some of Barrow's actions anyway. We decided then that, instead of making any resignations as Erskine wanted us to do there and then, we would raise the question at the forthcoming annual conference of the Party as to whether the 'Little Eight' federation should continue and, if the Party decided that it should not, then we would take whatever steps that we thought we should.

There was nothing really for us to discuss in the Cabinet because the proposed setting up of this 'Little Eight' Federation was being carried on independently of any Cabinet discussion. We had already accepted the principle of federation in London and we were only really working out the mechanics for the federal structure. So these delegates would meet every three or four months to discuss the structural proposals for the federation. What broke it up was the very last meeting when all they were supposed to do was sign their names to the document. As Premier, Barrow was at that meeting. We heard of the confusion at 'Sherbourne' only when Erskine telephoned us and told us he was leaving the government. We mounted a campaign against the breakdown of the federal discussions because we thought the federation meant a lot to Barbados, and because there was considerable support for the federation at that time. As I was the Minister of Trade and Industry, I knew that we had a number of applications for factories to be sited in Barbados, based on the proposal that we would have a "Little Eight" federation with a combined population of about two million.[1] This would have made the operation of these factories practical but they would have been completely impractical based on the Barbados population of 250,000.

Those who supported us at first, including Talma, were got at by Barrow and Tudor. When the Party accepted the resolution for independence for Barbados alone, Talma, Ward and myself moved a counter-resolution calling for independence within an Eastern Caribbean Federation; but none of the others supported it. Erskine notified me he had resigned, and I said, 'Well, I can't back down; I promised to support you and I've got to do it.' I handed in my resignation.

After the proposed federation of the 'Little Eight' broke up, we lost the combined market for specific industries which this population would have warranted. Barrow came along then with the proposals for CARICOM – the Customs Union with the other members of the Federation – which would then have opened the entire markets to each other. At the time, I thought it would have placed us at a disadvantage eventually. It would have been far better for us to have built up the 'Little Eight' as a single unit and develop a fairly strong basis and then go into a federation – we in one unit and Trinidad and Guyana in the other, and Jamaica, if they wanted to come in. There might have been problems with the partners in the 'Little Eight' and they might have taken the view that Barbados was getting the advantages and they were getting few. But we would have had to sit down and work out a compromise.

What really happened in the end was that the election which followed was based on the choice between the 'Little Eight' and Independence, and Barrow used the same argument that Bustamante had used in Jamaica, that, if we united with the Leewards and Windwards, the public funds from Barbados would have to be distributed among those small islands.[2] That is how Bustamante won the referendum in Jamaica. He told the people that, instead of spending Jamaican revenue to build up schools and repair roads in Jamaica, the money would have to be spent in Montserrat and Dominica which had few schools. The Jamaican public fell for it.

After the 'Little Eight' broke up, Barrow immediately called for Independence for Barbados. We supported the independence call provided that we had a general election first to let the people decide whether they wanted Barbados to have independence alone or independence within the 'Little Eight'. The 'Under Forties' (a group of public-spirited young men under forty), Ward, myself, the BLP and the Conservatives came out strongly in favour of the election before Independence. The government's attitude was that, if we went into this federation with those 'down-along' people, we would be reduced to an almshouse in a short while this, after we had spent eighteen months settling the federal structure! And we would then have to pick up government's funds and spend on the other islands. But the British government would have given a subvention at the beginning towards building up the infrastructure of the islands. In addition, they would have had to give an annual grant for public expenditure for a certain number of years. It had been agreed that this grant would continue for a specified period, although neither the period nor the amount had been specified. It would have been up to the Federation to decide how it could improve its own economy so that it would not have had to rely indefinitely on grants from Britain. The burden would not have had to fall on the Barbados treasury alone. Some of the leadership of the Leewards and Windwards gave some cause for alarm, but it was hoped that, in time, more responsible attitudes would have developed. Negotiations could have continued.

When Erskine Ward and I resigned from the Cabinet, it might have seemed that we wanted to challenge Barrow but, at the public meeting we held in Queen's Park after the resignations, we did not challenge him. There was a huge crowd there and everything was going well until I stupidly mentioned that we should start a new party and make Erskine leader. Half the people left and some DLP supporters started to throw stones on the Steel Shed.

I was among the few people in the Cabinet who knew Erskine Ward's career in the days when he first went into politics. Barrow did not know about him at all and the public at large did not either. It was a great loss to politics when he left (in 1932) to go on the Bench but I knew the support he had given to the Progressive movement. It was a little before my time but I knew of his contribution. He was a journalist and was Leader Writer for the *Advocate*. He edited the *Herald* when it was restarted by 'Chrissie' Brathwaite and Charlie Elder after the Wickham era. He was a lawyer. He knew all about sugar planting and agriculture generally and can be credited for reviving the sugar industry in this country in the 1960s. Ward was the man who really did the work for the Disturbances Commission. One day I heard him say that it was Charlie Elder who told them that they should have him on the Commission, because the conservatives did not want him. The Deane Commission Report, I understand, was written entirely by him, and all the proposals that were made were his. Sir George Deane was a member of the Legislative Council. His name was on the Commission but he was only a figurehead. I think he was a former Chief Justice in Belize, but obviously ineffectual as a politician or social reformer.

I could have justified my call to form another party but, to tell the truth, at my age I decided not to bother my head to go through all those troubles again as I was in my fifties then. This might be considered young as far as politics and world leadership are concerned. I found that Alexander Bustamante and Norman Manley *et al* went into politics in their forties and fifties, but I started the *Observer* at twenty-four and I got involved in a lot of things from the early days. As a matter of fact, one night when I was about twenty-five or twenty-six, I went down to St Andrew with Frank Holder to a meeting which Reverend Francis Godson was holding in connection with praedial larceny. He was trying to beg

Wynter Crawford in later life

the people not to interfere with their neighbours' crops. He asked me to come down to the meeting and report it in the *Observer* newspaper. Frank Holder was then Solicitor-General and he was a member for St Andrew in the House. On the way back he said, 'You know you're a damn fool; you should keep yourself quiet, keep the *Observer* like the *Advocate*, say nothing to offend the people, and make some money like everybody else.' I did not take his advice then but, by the time I was in my fifties, I had had enough.

Well, one might ask where I was heading. Why was I prepared to throw away my political life when office mattered so much? Let us say that the experience of Independence was comparatively recent in the West Indies and politicians clung to office. Now, you have examples all the time in other countries of people who went along with the policy of the government and later rejected it. Maybe resignation from office had never taken place in Barbados before but it can happen again. In some of these islands, for a number of years we had politicians who were entirely dependent for their economic existence on the money they got from parliament. This to a great extent explains why a lot of people in politics toe the line and why members of parliament do certain things or accept certain things. This was so even before party politics was fully developed. I felt that, as far as I was concerned, I was not dependent on politics for a living and I could express my opinions and act accordingly.

Notes

1   The population of the 'Little Eight' in 1965 was roughly 700,000 persons. Presumably Crawford was making a projection.
2   All the political parties had agreed at the Barbados Constitutional Conference held in June 1966 in London that Barbados should proceed to independence.

EPILOGUE

by

Dr. Delisle Crawford
(brother of W.A. Crawford)

The political career of the late Wynter Algernon Crawford officially ended in 1966. After the Annual Conference of the Democratic Labour Party (DLP) of that year, it followed naturally that Mr Crawford would submit his resignation as a matter of principle. Both he and the late Sir Erskine Ward were ardent federationists. It cannot be repeated too frequently that their position was independence for Barbados as a part of an independent West Indian Federation. Others, because it suited them, and because of its great appeal to the masses, dangled the exaggerated benefits of independence alone before the short-sighted members of the Party and, later, before the impressionable electorate. Indeed, one of the more ludicrous examples of the concept of benefits that would be derived from independence alone was exhibited by a newspaper vendor who came into my office the day after Independence celebrations in a most jubilant mood. He announced to me that he was finished working. When I enquired about the source of his new found wealth, he exclaimed: 'Doc, I done working. We independent now!' I must add that some years after I saw him selling newspaper again on Bay Street.

Many of us who are yet alive to and are aware of the geo-political changes taking place around the world must be saddened to see that, thirty years after independence, thanks to the shortsightedness and "big fish in little pond" mentality of many Caribbean leaders, these West Indian mini-states are still floundering in the sea of political uncertainty.

It is a fact of history that Mr Crawford and other members of his Congress Party merged with the Democratic Labour Party. It is also a fact of history that this combination, as the Democratic Labour Party, won the 1961 election using what had been mainly the Manifesto of Mr

Crawford's Congress Party. So successful was this programme that the DLP became entrenched in the minds of the electorate in Mr Crawford's constituency of St Philip, and, so, when Mr. Crawford offered himself as an independent candidate in the pre-Independence election, he was defeated.

During the intervening years (between 1966 and 1993), Mr Crawford remained ardently interested in the affairs of Barbados and the Caribbean. When he travelled overseas, he always tried to interest industrialists and tourism officials in coming to Barbados. Mr Crawford was consulted by politicians and political aspirants of all ages on matters of political and constitutional importance as they arose. Even more gratifying to him must have been the fact that students from many countries of the Caribbean and further afield who were involved in political science research consulted with him.

It should be noted that the limited reference to the important issue of Federation in this volume is entirely due to the "question and answer" method of its origin, and certainly does not convey Mr Crawford's deep and abiding interest in a West Indian Federation.

Wynter Crawford, both as Editor and Publisher of the *Barbados Observer* for over forty years, and as a politician representing the parish of St Philip and the interest of Barbados in parliament over a period of twenty-six years, made an outstanding contribution to the political, constitutional and economic advancement of Barbados – indeed, a contribution almost without parallel.

Mr Crawford was awarded the CHB in 1980 for his services to this country. Ironically enough, it was awarded **not** during the regime of the party (the DLP) to which he had brought the full benefits of his considerable acumen in political affairs but by the Government of the day, headed by the late J.M.G.M. Adams, the son of the late Sir Grantley Adams, with whom Mr. Crawford was invariably at loggerheads.

It is worthy of mention that among Mr Crawford's outstanding proposals which eventually became reality were the Hilton Hotel, the Flour Mill and the East Coast Road, the construction of which he had tirelessly promoted since the 1940s.

APPENDIX

Wynter Crawford's Major Parliamentary Interventions,
1940–1961

I The Sugar Industry (workers, peasant cane farmers, etc)

Question, 21 May 1940: Unemployment of Sugar Boilers
Question, 21 May 1940: Government acquisition of sugar estates
Address, 25 June 1940: Certification for sugar boilers
Question, 1 October 1940: Distribution of sugar preference
Question, 6 May 1941: Peasant proprietors selling canes to sugar factories
Speech, 3 June 1941: Purchase of boiler and other equipment
Speech, 24 June 1941: Non-Shipment of Fancy Molasses Crop
Speech, 12 August 1941: Sale of peasants' canes to sugar factories
Speech, 19 August 1941: Sale of peasants' canes to sugar factories/absentee proprietors
Speech, 2 September 1941: Sale of peasants' canes to sugar factories/absentee proprietors
Speech, 9 September 1941: Sale of peasants' canes to sugar factories/absentee proprietors
Speech, 16 September 1941: Select committee to consider and report on Bill to fix minimum price per ton for sugar canes (declined membership)
Speech, 30 September 1941: Selling of canes by peasant proprietors/absentee proprietors
Address, 22 January 1942: Sugar boilers
Question, 30 June 1942: Prohibition of manufacture of syrup during reaping season
Question, 8 September 1942: Social welfare for workers in sugar industry
Speech, 3 November 1942: Minimum price for sugar canes
Question, 23 February 1943: Prices of canes to peasant growers
Speech, 8 June 1943: Increased cost of carriage of canes to sugar factories
Speech, 29 June 1943: Increased cost of the carriage of canes to sugar factories
Speech, 30 January 1945: Minimum price for sugar canes Bill
Speech, 13 February 1945: Employment of children on sugar estates
Address, 31 July 1945: Call for nationalisation of the sugar industry
Proposed Bill, 1 June 1948: 'An Act to enforce the wage rates for the sugar industry for the year 1948–49'
Question, 10 August 1948: Recovery of individual factories, etc., during the manufacture of the sugar cane crop for 1948
Question, 18 January 1949: Sugar cane crop, 1948

Question, 8 February 1949: Prices paid for peasants' canes at last crop

Motion, 13 December 1949: Sugar talks in the UK – an amendment of an address by E.D. Mottley

Address, 24 January 1950: BWI sugar producers to accept proposals of UK Ministry of Food

Question, 23 March 1950: Prices paid for peasants' canes, 1948, 1949 crops

Address, 9 September 1952: Cane prices

Address, 30 June 1953: Housing for sugar workers

Address, 5 January 1954: The sugar industry, interests of small holders/producers and need for regulation of the industry

Address, 11 May 1954: Low prices paid to small cane farmers during the current crop season

Address, 26 October 1954: Establishment of a sugar refinery in Barbados and procurement of market for surplus BWI sugar in Africa

Address, 8 March 1955: Committee of enquiry into unequal distribution of profits from the sugar industry

Question, 1 May 1956: Low prices paid for canes by sugar factories during the current crop

Address, 28 May 1958: Unjust treatment of peasant farmers and small cane growers for the 1958 crop

Speech, 17 February 1959: Resolution re report on sugar industry by McKenzie

Resolution, 29 March 1960: Investigation into all phases of the sugar industry in Barbados

Resolution, 10 January 1961: Investigation into all phases of the Barbados sugar industry (repeat of March 8, 1960)

Speech, 4 July 1961: Debate on registered sugar factories' Smoke Control Bill

Speech, 29 August 1961: Investigation into the Barbados sugar industry

II Overpopulation/Unemployment/Emigration

Speech, 16 July 1940: Unemployment

Speech, 14 January 1941: Loan to Barbados Settlement Company Ltd.

Address, 3 June 1941: Settlement of Barbadians in British Guiana

Speech, 3 June 1941: Employment of artisans in St. Peter and St. Lucy

Speech, 3 June 1941: Recruiting of Barbadian labourers for work on USA Defence Bases

Speech, 2 September 1941: Additional housing accommodation at Vieux Fort, St Lucia

Question, 3 February 1942: Advisability of sending Barbadian workers to work in Panama

Address, 21 April 1942: Advisability of sending Barbadian workers to work in British Guiana

Speech, 12 May 1942: Barbadians refused admission at Trinidad

Speech, 18 August 1942: Unemployment

Question, 19 January 1943: Employment for Barbados merchant seamen

Question, 2 March 1943: Employment for Barbadians at US Bases in the Caribbean

Address, 30 March 1943: Employment of Barbadians in USA

Question, 15 June 1943: Employment of Barbadian workers on farms in USA

Speech, 16 November 1943: Employment of workers on extension of work at Tobago Aerodrome (motion withdrawn)

Address, 21 August 1945: Scheme for Barbadian workers to settle in British Guiana, British Honduras or any other colonies in the British West Indies

Address, 2 December 1947: Scheme for obtaining employment for Barbadian workers in USA

Address, 9 December 1947: Secondment of a 'labour officer' to help arrange deployment of Barbadian workers to USA

Address, 11 May 1948: Call for delegation to visit the USA to investigate possibilities of obtaining employment for Barbadian workers in USA

Address, 11 May 1948: Call for a programme of public works to reduce unemployment, including airport at Seawell, wharf walls, construction of elementary and secondary schools and laying of water mains

Address, 15 June 1948: Hostility of the UK Government to arrival of skilled British West Indian workers in the UK

Address, 6 July 1948: Shooting of unarmed sugar estate workers in British Guiana who were endeavouring to improve their wages and conditions of work

Address, 10 August 1948: Possibility of Barbadian workers emigrating to Liberia

Question, 17 August 1948: Possibility of securing reasonable prices for construction materials in the UK for proposed public works programme to relieve unemployment in Barbados

Address/Presenting Report, 12 October 1948: Report of the Select Committee appointed to draft a reply to His Excellency's Message No. 13/1948, relating to unemployment relief works

Address, 21 December 1948: Barbadians to settle in Liberia

Address, 15 March 1949: Entry of West Indians to work in the USA

Address, 26 May 1949: Acute labour shortage in Bermuda; possibility of sending Barbadian workers to gain employment there

Address, 5 February 1950: Representation of Barbadians and West Indians in Panama

Address, 19 February 1952: Appreciation to US Congressman Clayton Powell re 'McCarran Bill'

Question, 3 February 1953: Possibility of sending agricultural workers to St Croix, USVI

Address, 1 June 1954: Possibility of sending Barbadian workers to work on Canadian farms

Speech, 2 November 1954: Emigration to England

Address, 22 March 1955: Advance from Sugar Industry Price Stabilization Reserve Fund to implement system for 5,000 Barbadian workers to obtain employment in the UK under contract

Address, 28 May 1958: Sending Barbadian workers to help reap cane crop in Suriname

Resolution, 10 January 1961: Investigatory Committee to look into operations of Farm Labour Programme

Resolution, 20 June 1961: Quota restrictions for emigrants to the USA after Federation and Independence

III Social Security/National Insurance

Speech, 13 August 1940: Pension for William Griffith
Question, 4 February 1941: Assistance to social welfare department
Speech, 27 May 1941: Compensation to Rollins Boyce/proposed implementation of Ontario model of social welfare – a recommendation of West India Royal Commission
Speech, 8 July 1941: Compensation to Urban Goddard
Speech, 29 July 1941: Ex gratia grant to Carlotta Bedford
Speech, 29 July 1941: Grant to Eleanor Brathwaite
Speech, 30 September 1941: Workmen's Compensation Bill – called for inclusion of agricultural workers in legislation
Speech, 28 October 1941: Workmen's Compensation Bill
Speech, 11 November 1941: Workmen's Compensation Bill
Speech, 9 December 1941: Workmen's Compensation Bill
Speech, 21 July 1942: Workmen's Compensation Bill
Speech, 18 August 1942: Spencer Pension Bill
Question, 27 October 1942: Gratuity for Evan Archibald Alleyne
Speech, 16 February 1943: Inconvenience to old age pensioners in St Lucy
Question, 23 September 1943: Compensation for dependents of workers lost at sea
Speech, 16 November 1943: Subsistence Allowance to Benjamin Skeete
Speech, 18 April 1944: Parochial Pension Bill
Address, 10 October 1944: Low level of old age pensions
Address, 10 April 1945: Social Security Scheme
Speech, 12 June 1945: The Old Age Pension (Amendment) Bill
Address, 31 July 1945: Increase in remuneration of payment and enquiry officers
Question, 21 August 1945: Operations of Barbados Welfare Ltd.
Address, 21 October 1947: On the establishment of a joint contributory system of social security for Barbados
Proposed Bill, 6 January 1948: To authorise the Sugar Industry Agricultural Bank to grant gratuity to legal representatives of Norman Lisle Roach (deceased)
Proposed Bill, 6 April 1948: Second reading – to authorise the Sugar Industry Agricultural Bank to grant gratuity to legal representatives of Norman Lisle Roach (deceased)
Address, 21 December 1948: Establishment of a Social Security Scheme for Barbados
Address, 24 October 1950: Establishment of Social Security Scheme for Barbados
Question, 8 July 1952: Old age pensions
Question, 3 February 1953: Compensation for dependents of the late Louis Jordan
Address, 30 June 1953: A Comprehensive Social Security Scheme for Barbados, including an Insurance Scheme

Address, 5 January 1954: Comprehensive Social Security Scheme for Barbados
Address, 28 May 1958: Establishment of system of social security, and a joint
    Contributory Provident Fund

IV Education

Question, 28 May 1940: Free supply of school books and stationery for
    school children
Question, 30 June, 1940: Water borne latrine for St Philip's Church Girls'
    School
Speech, 13 August 1940: Increased salaries for teachers
Speech, 24 September 1940: Milk and biscuits for school children
Speech, 1 October 1940: Additional accommodation at Government Indus-
    trial Schools
Speech, 4 March 1941: Education policy, with reference to the Report of the
    West India Royal Commission
Speech, 4 March 1941: Further accommodation for the teaching of Science
Speech, 18 March 1941: Annual estimates, from milk to teacher-training
Speech, 6 May 1941: Calling for fully qualified Director of Education
Speech, 6 May 1941: West India Royal Commission recommendations on
    Education
Speech, 27 May 1941: Quality of milk supplied to school children
Speech, 8 July 1941: Erection of additional latrines at Wesley Hall Boys' School
Address, 3 February 1942: Increased salaries for assistant teachers at public
    elementary schools
Question, 17 March 1942: Training of teachers, etc.
Speech/Question, 24 March 1942: Increase in salaries for teachers of Rawle
    Institute
Speech, 18 August 1942: Teachers Pension (Amendment) Bill
Question, 8 September 1942: Free supply of books for school children
Speech, 26 January 1943: Education (Amendment) Bill
Speech, 23 March 1943: Education estimates
Speech, 17 August 1943: Address re free compulsory education
Speech, 1 March 1944: On the quality of American universities and education
Speech, 20 June 1944: Education (Amendment) Bill
Question, 10 October 1944: Organisation of primary schools
Speech, 9 January 1945: Supplementary Resolution for Educational Purposes
Speech, 20 March 1945: The colonial estimates – education
Speech, 17 July 1945: The Education Bill
Question, 26 April 1949: Restoration of scholarships from primary schools to
    Queen's College
Question, 4 October 1949: Terms and conditions of service for teaching staff at
    Government Industrial Schools
Question, 4 October 1949: Ration allowance for staff at Government Indus-
    trial Schools
Resolution, 8 March 1960: Government to provide more secondary school
    places and the regulation of private secondary schools

Resolution, 10 January 1961: Secondary school education in Barbados (repeat of resolution of March 8, 1960)

Question, 10 January 1961: Establishment of Law Faculty of UCWI at Codrington College

V Labour Issues

Question, 1 October 1940: Treatment of non-commissioned officer of the police force

Speech, 26 November 1940: Installation of telephones at police posts

Question, 17 December 1940: Harbour police grievances

Speech, 21 January 1941: Labour officer's department

Question, 4 March 1941: Restoration of police leave

Speech, 4 March 1941: Status of conciliation boards

Speech, 18 March 1941: Police service

Speech, 27 May 1941: Harbour police

Speech, 3 June 1941: Scale of wages for Public Works Department

Speech, 3 June 1941: Storage of petrol at police stations

Speech, 8 July 1941: Police Social Literary and Athletic Club

Speech, 10 June 1941: Additional war bonus to civil servants; called for additional 10 per cent for agricultural labourers and certain classes of government employees

Speech, 29 July 1941: Police Social Literary and Athletic Club

Speech, 10 March 1942: Terms and conditions of work for government messengers

Speech, 10 March 1942: Terms and conditions of work for postmen

Speech, 17 March 1942: Police service

Speech, 17 March 1942: Prisons

Speech, 17 March 1942: The 'Dodds'

Speech, 5 May 1942: Dissatisfaction in the police force

Question, 30 June 1942: Dissatisfaction in civil service

Question, 27 October 1942: Conditions of work for workers at Bowmanston Pumping Station

Speech, 16 March 1943: Police estimates

Speech, 4 July 1944: Employees in government departments

Speech, 11 July 1944: New scale of wages for government employees

Speech, 22 August 1944: Civil Establishment (Miscellaneous Provisions) Bill

Speech, 29 August 1944: Civil Establishment (Miscellaneous Provisions) Bill

Speech, 5 September 1944: Civil Establishment (Miscellaneous Provisions) Bill

Speech, 12 September 1944: Civil Establishment (Miscellaneous Provisions) Bill

Speech, 19 September 1944: Civil Establishment (Miscellaneous Provisions) Bill

Speech, 26 September 1944: Supplementary Resolution granting increases to staff of government departments

Question, 14 October 1947: Publication of the Calver Report on the Barbados Police Force

Address, 31 August 1948: Salaries paid to official reporters [of the House of Assembly]

Address, 7 September 1948: Dissatisfaction amongst members of the public service, and calling for making available remuneration entitled to them as a result of the investigation conducted by Mr Adams

Address, 13 December 1949: Payment of workers who work on public holidays

Question, 31 January 1950: Pay for overtime work for Waterworks employees

Question, 23 March 1950: Artisans at Seawell runway

Address, 20 May 1952: Labour Welfare Fund

Question, 20 May 1952: Conditions at quarries

Speech, 19 January 1953: Grievances of sugar plantation overseers

Address, 29 May 1956: Harmonization of terms and conditions of service for employees of local government bodies and the civil service

Resolution, 3 February 1959: Increased travelling allowances for postal carriers.

VI Peasant Agriculture/Land Settlement

Question, 25 June 1940: Land settlement in Barbados

Address, 29 April 1941: Assistance to peasant landholders in increasing food production

Address, 3 June 1941: Increasing the number of peasant holdings by acquisition of sugar estates

Question, 28 July 1942: Dissatisfaction among cotton producers

Speech, 18 August 1942: Extending the scope of the Peasants Loan Bank

Speech, 6 October 1942: On Bill to establish factory to process locally grown vegetables

Speech, 15 December 1942: Peasants Loan Bank

Speech, 16 February 1943: Restriction on the use of imported fertilisers

Speech, 29 February 1944: Extension of Peasants' Loan Bank

Question, 10 October 1944: On desirability of making more land available to the bulk of the population

Speech, 14 August 1945: Reform of the Peasants Loan Bank

Address, 30 June 1953: Provision of lands from Summervale and Dodds plantations for housing and experimental profit farms

VII Food Supply/Cost of Living

Speech, 15 October 1940: Importation and distribution of foodstuffs

Question, 18 March 1941: Shortage of maize and cornmeal

Speech, 10 June 1941: Shortage of maize and cornmeal

Speech, 24 June 1941: Shortage of maize and cornmeal

Address, 9 September 1941: Rising cost of living; proposal for government to distribute essential foodstuffs

Speech, 16 December 1941: Opposition to increases in price of edible oil

Question, 21 April 1942: Government action to reduce cost of living

Address, 23 February 1954: Shortage of pickled pork products in Barbados

Address, 10 April 1958: Establishment of committee to investigate the abnormally high cost of living

VIII War Measures

Speech, 16 September 1941: Expenses in connection with the present emergency

Address, 16 December 1941: Expression of sympathy and support to American people re attack on Pearl Harbour and same to president and peoples of the Soviet Union

Speech, 16 December 1941: Expenses of the present emergency

Address, 3 February 1942: 10 per cent increase on salaries for all public servants and teachers in receipt of war bonus and 10 per cent increase on salaries of all public servants and teachers not in receipt of war bonus

Speech, 30 June 1942: Increase of war bonus for civil servants

Speech, 7 July 1942: Subsidisation of essential foodstuffs

Speech, 21 July 1942: Indian corn and the food situation

Speech, 21 July 1942: Production of cassava flour

Speech, 11 August 1942: Present emergency expenses

Speech, 8 September 1942: Subsidisation of certain foodstuffs

Speech, 13 October 1942: Supplementary emergency expenses

Address, 3 November 1942: Increase of rice ration

Speech, 1 February 1944: Expenses in connection with present emergency

Speech, 8 May 1945: Address in respect of the cessation of hostilities in Europe

Speech, 14 August 1945: Representation of the West Indies at Peace Conference

IX The Fishing Industry

Address, 25 June 1940: Establishment of facilities for canning of fish

Question, June 1940: Advancing of sea-egg season

Question, 16 July 1940: The sea-egg close season

Question, 4 March 1941: Condition of Megs Channel, St Philip

Question, 29 April 1941: Plight of fishermen of St Philip, with respect to Megs Channel

Address, 22 January 1942: The fishing industry

Address, 22 January 1942: Megs Channel in St Philip

Speech, 3 November 1942: Rehabilitation of the fishing industry

Speech, 3 November 1942: Megs Channel

Address, 12 January 1943: Widening and deepening of Megs Channel

Speech, 9 March 1943: Fisheries Regulation (Amendment) Bill

Speech, 3 October 1944: Rehabilitation and extension of the fishing industry

Question, 10 July 1951: Fishermen at Megs Channel and Skeetes Bay

Address, 8 June 1954: Raising the ceiling of unsecured loans to fishermen

Address, 8 November 1955: Request of $20,000 from government to fishermen who sustained losses during the recent hurricane

Address, 14 August 1956: Assistance to operators/owners of fishing craft with sails to convert them into mechanised units

X St Philip (Crawford's constituency)

Address, 3 February 1942: Second grade school for St Philip from E.J. Hutchinson Trust Fund

Question, 22 June 1948: Restoration of KGVM Park, St Philip, as a playing field and recreational centre

Question, 26 April 1949: Police force and parishioners of St Philip

Question, 13 December 1949: Bus service to St Philip for school children

Question, 13 December 1949: Supply of fresh water to St Philip

Question, 5 January 1950: Public baths and latrines in St Philip

Question, 7 March 1950: Establishment of branch of Public Library in St Philip

Proposed Bill, 6 May 1952: 'An Act to authorise the vestry of the parish of St Philip ... to sell the building known as The Isolation Hospital'

Proposed Bill, 6 May 1952: 'An Act to authorise the vestry of the parish of St Philip to provide exhibitions at any first grade school in Barbados of a total not exceeding £140 per annum'

Address, 1 June 1954: The establishment of a secondary school in the parish of St Philip

Question, 1 June 1954: Allocation of standposts for the parish of St Philip

Address, 15 February 1955: Conversion of Princess Margaret School into a bilateral school

Question, 3 May 1955: Construction of access road for fishermen at Long Bay Beach, St Philip

Question, 3 May 1955: Acquisition of water main from Long Bay corner to Sam Lord's Castle for use of householders

XI Public Works

Speech, 8 October 1940: Repairs to government buildings

Speech, 5 November 1940: Repairs to government buildings

Speech, 31 December 1940: Supplementary vote, lunatic asylum

Speech, 18 March 1941: Annual estimates, made link between maintenance of salaries and voter qualifications

Speech, 17 May 1941: Public Works (Amendment) Bill

Speech, 22 September 1941: Construction of reservoir at Castle Grant

Speech, 9 September 1941: Erection of new ward at lunatic asylum

Speech, 9 September 1941: Repair of roads at Bulkeley and Andrews factories and Parris Hill

Speech, 25 November 1941: Construction of runway at Seawell

Speech, 25 November 1941: Repairing roads in St Andrew

Speech, 3 February 1942: Repair of approach road to Seawell Airport

Question, 2 June 1942: Widening Orange Street, other streets in Speightstown

Speech, 18 August 1942: Clearing and levelling lands behind Queen's College and Combermere School

Speech, 3 November 1942: Mental hospital

Speech, 12 January 1943: Need for water supply in tenantries

Speech, 30 March 1943: Supplementary vote for waterworks pumping expenses

Speech, 30 November 1943: Miscellaneous services

Speech, 25 January 1944: Vote for repair of damaged roads in St Joseph

Speech, 14 March 1944: Subsidies and grants

Speech, 25 July 1944: Deplorable condition of tenantry roads
Speech, 27 March 1945: Department of highways and transport Bill
Speech, 17 July 1945: Widening or deepening of channels on Windward Coast
Speech, 31 July 1945: Public Health (Amendment) Bill
Question, 20 January 1948: Rehabilitation of Whim Road, St Peter
Question, 7 March 1950: Constitution Swamp, East Coast Road
Address, 28 April 1953: Housing, road construction, siting of tenantries, etc.,

XII Public Utilities

Address, 11 November 1941: Call for commission to enquire into operations
    of Barbados Electric Supply Corporation
Speech, 25 November 1941 and 9 December 1941: Need for government con-
    trol of utilities to ensure that subscribers are not penalised by defective meters
Address, 21 April 1942: Appointment of Commission of Enquiry into opera-
    tions of Barbados Electric Supply Corporation
Speech, 1 February 1944: Public Library (Amendment) Bill
Question, 7 March 1950: Erection of more waiting sheds at bus terminals
Address, 10 April 1958: Dissatisfaction over recent revisions of omnibus fares

XIII Public Health

Speech, 29 April 1941: General Hospital (Amendment) Bill
Speech, 6 May 1941: Appointment of Night Sister at General Hospital/called
    for greater transparency in affairs of Boards
Speech, 11 August 1942: Public Health (Amendment) Bill
Speech, 18 August 1942: Public Health (Amendment) Bill
Address, 23 February 1954: Shortage of medical doctors, particularly at night

XIV Housing

Speech, 11 February 1941: Need for low-income housing
Speech, 24 March 1943: The Housing Board Vote
Speech, 27 July 1943: Articles of the Housing Board
Question, 7 March 1950: Introduction of Rent Restriction Board
Address, 9 September 1952: Houses in Government Housing Scheme

XV Judicial Establishment/Judicial Reform

Speech, 27 May 1941: Jury expenses
Speech, 24 June 1941: Judicial Establishment (Amendment) Bill
Address, 12 August 1941: Establishment of Court of Criminal Appeal
Speech, 26 August 1941: Chief Judge and Common Law Officers (Amend-
    ment) Bill
Speech, 12 March 1942: Appointment of additional judges, etc.
Speech, 29 June 1943: Judicial Establishment (Amendment) Bill
Speech, 26 October 1943: Abolition of the Grand Jury
Question, 18 January 1944: Professional qualifications for police magistrates

XVI The Anglican Church

Speech, 25 June 1940: Absence of Anglican clergymen from their cures
Speech, 26 November 1940: Anglican Church (Barbados) Amendment Bill
Speech, 17 March 1942: The Anglican Church – expenditure on and policy of
Speech, 17 August 1943: Dis-establishment of the Anglican Church
Proposed Bill, 28 September 1943: To disestablish the Anglican Church
Proposed Bill, 23 May 1944: To disestablish and disendow the Anglican Church
  of this island
Speech, 22 August 1944: Disestablishment of the Anglican Church
Speech, 19 September 1944: On the Anglican Church
Proposed Bill, 21 December 1948: To disestablish the Anglican Church
Speech, 28 June 1955: On Anglican Church Bill

XVII Industry/Manufacturing

Speech, 13 March 1941: Manufacturing of oleomargarine in Barbados
Speech, 10 June 1941: Call for local maize, corn meal industry
Speech, 12 August 1941: British Union Oil Company Gas (Facilities for Development) Bill
Question, 21 April 1942: Production of cassava flour
Speech, 18 August 1942: Production of cassava flour
Speech, 18 August 1942: Increased production of cassava flour
Speech, 15 September 1942: Erection of cassava and potato factory
Speech, 24 November 1942: Manufacture of alpargatas (sandals) in Barbados
Speech, 27 July 1943: Resolution to meet the additional cost of cassava processing facility
Proposed Bill, 12 October 1948: The Industries Aid and Encouragement Act, 1948
Proposed Bill, 21 December 1948: Industries Aid and Encouragement Act, 1949
Question, 7 March 1950: Hotel Aid Bill
Question, 24 October 1950: Establishment of a flour mill for Barbados
Address, 23 February 1954: Protection for recently established textile, shirt industries in Barbados
Address, 8 January 1955: Agricultural and industrial development programme for Barbados
Address, 8 March 1955: Establishing a metal industry in Barbados and the BWI
Address, 29 May 1956: Possibility of establishing aluminum plant in area, with the governments of Jamaica, British Guiana and Trinidad
Speech, 12 August 1958: Barbados Development (Amendment) Bill
Address, 2 September 1958: Expansion of local poultry industry
Resolution, 23 February 1959: Expansion of local poultry industry
Resolution, 17 January 1961: Establishment of a flour mill in Barbados
Resolution, 22 August 1961: Banning export of scrap metal from the BWI Federation to facilitate establishment of steel mill to manufacture iron and steel goods

XVIII   Travel/Tourism

Speech, 7 July1942: British West Indian Airways Agreement
Address, 7 July 1942: Inter-island air travel
Address, 6 May 1952: Withdrawal of 'Lady Boats' of Canadian National Steamship Ltd.
Resolution, 5 May 1959: Conference of airlines for reduction of air transport costs with particular reference to the tourist industry

XIX Government Revenue

Speech, 4 March 1941: Revenue in Aid Bill
Speech, 4 March 1941: Petroleum (Amendment) Bill
Speech, 4 March 1941: Miscellaneous Taxation (Amendment) Bill
Speech, 25 March 1941: Rates of Income Tax Bill/inequitable distribution of the tax burden
Speech, 16 September 1941: Refund of customs duty to A.S. Bryden
Speech, 27 March 1942: House Inspection Taxes
Speech, 30 June 1942: Rates of Income Tax
Speech, 24 November 1942: Customs Tariff (Amendment) Bill
Speech, 26 October 1943: Government setting up its own printing office
Speech, 27 February 1945: Miscellaneous Taxation Bill
Speech, 13 March 1945: Customs Tariff (Amendment) Bill
Speech, 15 March 1945: Committee of supply/The colonial estimates
Speech, 14 September 1945: Rates of Income Tax Bill
Address, 14 October 1947, 11 November 1947: 'the dollar crisis'
Address, 8 February 1949: Taxation of government-owned properties
Question, 26 April 1949: National debt
Question, 1 June 1954: Operations of the Token Import Scheme
Question, 1 May 1956: Funds invested aboard as of March 31, 1956

XX Constitutional and Political Issues

Question, 16 July 1940: Release of the political prisoners (the 1937 rioters)
Speech, 10 June 1941: Old Representative System vs Crown Colony Government
Speech, 9 September 1941: The electoral system
Speech, 9 December 1941: Attitude of the Legislative Council: in relation to infringement of rights to pass Money Bills
Speech, 17 February 1942: Executive Committee (Amendment) Bill
Speech, 21 April 1942: Representation of the People (Amendment) Bill
Speech, 4 May 1943: The Representation of the People (Amendment) Bill
Speech, 7 December 1943: Council's Amendments to The Representation of the People Act
Speech, 21 March 1944: Representation of the People (Amendment) Bill
Speech, 18 January 1944: Representation of the People (Amendment) Bill
Speech, 1 March 1944: Representation of the People (Amendment) Bill
Resolution, 13 January 1959: Removal of word 'Colonial' from the title, 'Member, Colonial Parliament'

Resolution, 29 March 1960: Ending of racial discrimination in Barbados

XXI House of Assembly
(conduct of business, etc.)

Speech, 28 May 1940: Lack of response to questions asked
Speech, 1 October 1940: Unsatisfactory treatment of questions raised
Speech, 1 October 1940: Lack of financial accountability
Speech, 14 January 1941: Procedures, House of Assembly
Speech, 25 February 1941: Rules of the House
Question, 4 March 1941: Delay in obtaining replies to questions
Speech, 3 June 1941: Slow rate of replies to questions
Speech, 11 January 1944: Prolongation of the General Assembly Bill

XXII Legislation

Speech, 29 April 1941: Estate and Succession Duties Bill
Bill, 21 April 1942: To amend Shop Closing Act
Speech, 18 August 1942: Meetings of Parochial and Statutory Bodies (Admission of the Press) Bill
Speech, 23 February 1943: Liquor Licenses (Amendment) Bill
Question, 18 January 1944: Publication in press of amounts of death duties on estates
Speech, 13 June 1944: The Shops Bill
Speech, 10 July 1945: Shops Closing Bill
Address, 10 April 1958: Legislation for benefits to women during pregnancy and confinement
Resolution, 23 February 1959: Maternity leave/benefits for women

XXIII Federation/Regional Integration

Speech, 5 April 1948: Montego Bay Conference
Address, 7 September, 21 December 1948: Annual interchange of schoolchildren on holiday to promote BWI unity
Address, 10 June 1952: Establishment of a West Indian State Bank (amendment)
Address, 2 September 1952: BWI Closer Union
Speech, 10 February 1953: BWI Federation
Address, 5 January 1954: Establishment of a BWI State Bank
Address, 25 January 1955: Establishment of a BWI State Bank
Resolution, 20 June 1961: Establishment of a Custom Union between Barbados and Leewards and Windwards

XXIV International Solidarity

Address, 23 February 1943: 5th anniversary of the Red Army
Speech, 23 February 1943: Tribute to the Red Army
Resolutions, 3 February 1948: Sympathy to government of India on death of Gandhi

Address, 28 April 1953: Contribution to legal defence of Jomo Kenyatta,
    Fanuel Odele, members of the Kenya African Union
Address, 28 April 1953: Concern over repression of population in Kenya
Speech, 29 September 1953: Repressive measures taken against Kenya native
    population

INDEX

MARCUS GARVEY BORN 17th AUGUST 188_

DIED 10th JUNE 1940